Pastor Eddie Rodriguez' ministerial trajectory speaks to the awesomeness of God's divine purpose exhibited via the conduit of a life committed to the centrality of Christ, the preaching of the full Gospel and sharing of the grace-filled love of God to everyone, without exception. His wisdom and personal journey carries an anointing to impact this emerging generation with the necessary tools to change the world.

Rev. Samuel Rodriguez

I have known Eddie Rodriguez since we were teenagers. We were both from the Bronx in New York. We were both part of the same congregation: Thessalonica Christian Church.

He started young in the ministry. He came from a pastoral home. By the time he was twenty, he and his wife, Martha, were already having revivals everywhere; not only in the US, but in Latin America and the Caribbean. Early in life, he was exposed to many denominational leaders, and that shaped him in his ministerial career. Eddie drew from so many seasoned leaders while he was still a young minister.

In "Called...Now What?" he shares his years of experience as a husband, father, Pastor, District Superintendent and community leader. He shares, not what he has heard, but what he has lived throughout his many years in the ministry. This book will serve as an inspiration to young and old ministers alike.

Many pastors and ecclesiastical leaders leave the ministry or go into retirement with their amazing stories. Many times, these stories are left untold. Eddie Rodriguez, once a teenage preacher, will bless the lives of a new generation of ministers with his story throughout this book.

We salute Eddie for a great work.

>Nino Gonzalez
>Pastor of Calvary City Church
>District Superintendent
>Florida Multicultural District

In the pastorate, it takes many years to grow and mature. There are certain areas and processes that are avoided when you have the help of a mentor; and that is what makes this book so useful!

Pastor Eddie Rodriguez is a man experienced in brokenness. He has been to the bottom of the abyss, and he has climbed victoriously to the mountain top. It is because of these experiences that he shares the following words. "I want to build a fence on the edge of the cliff rather than build a hospital at the bottom of the cliff. I want to prepare and warn the Called about what awaits them."

The moment I started reading "Called...Now What?" something stirred in the depth of my inner being. I felt relieved to know that now others will not have to go through what he already has. This manual is practical in the application of its concepts, and it is a healing agent that has components for self-examination. If you become brave enough to look inside and recognize where you have failed, the questionnaires will help you to position yourself correctly in all areas of your being, as well as in your doing.

I remember a story Pastor Eddie shared one day about how he had handled a division in his church. My response was, "Pastor, I'm not that good." He replied, "Neither am I. I'm just dead…"

This book is deep. Be prepared to receive pearls extracted from the solitude, the experience, the pain, the joy, and the very life of two young people who gave their strength and their better years to the Lord. Both Pastors Eddie and Martha have been processed for our benefit. Receive this gift from a couple who has learned on the battlefield, the deepest and most beneficial secrets of the war; and from pastors who do not hinder God with ego, so that their Lord can be glorified.

We value and appreciate what this book means for young pastors who are just starting out; and for the not-so-young that recognize that one can never stop learning. Thank you for freeing those who read your book of the pathological, chronic, delayed, exaggerated or masked-grief that ministers can potentially experience in their journey.

You have our respect and admiration because of your faithfulness. You are both a blessing to all!!

Thank you, Pastor Eddie, for the privilege of translating your book.

Claribel Hernández Colon

CALLED!
Now What?

EDDIE RODRIGUEZ

All rights reserved. No part of this publication may be reproduced, distributed, or transmitted in any form or by any means, including photocopying, recording, or other electronic or mechanical methods, without the prior written permission of the publisher, except in the case of brief quotations embodied in critical reviews and certain other noncommercial uses permitted by copyright law.

Scripture quotations from American Standard Version (1901) The American Standard Version of the Holy Bible, first published in 1901.

Scripture quotations from The Authorized (King James) Version. Rights in the Authorized Version in the United Kingdom are vested in the Crown. Reproduced by permission of the Crown's patentee, Cambridge University Press

THE HOLY BIBLE, NEW INTERNATIONAL VERSION®, NIV® Copyright © 1973, 1978, 1984, 2011 by Biblica, Inc.® Used by permission. All rights reserved worldwide.

Copyright © 2017 Eddie Rodriguez
All rights reserved.

ISBN-13: 978-0692947289
ISBN-10: 0692947280

For information about special discounts available for bulk purchases, contact the author at eddierodriguez212@yahoo.com

I Dedicate This Book to My Lovely Wife, Martha

I'm the visionary and she fills in all the details.
I see in her a true minister.
Her tireless spirit is admirable,
and I get tired just looking at her.
She's been my companion in this journey;
a journey that without her unconditional love,
would have been impossible.

To My 3 Awesome Kids

Edward Jr., Darlene and Michelle
You have been in this journey with me
and have survived and thrived.
I am truly a blessed and proud father.

I also dedicate this work to my grandkids, Joey, David, Danielle, Isabella, Giuliana, Jeremiah and Jason. That these truths may guide your journey.

To My Dad Pastor Nelson Rodriguez

You are a perfect example of a man
that loves Jesus, his word and people.
He's not only my dad,
but my pastor and mentor in life.

Acknowledgements

I want to give my heartfelt thanks to a very precious lady, Roz Perez. Without her help, this would have been an impossible task for me. She has given of her valuable time and expertise, with so much love and dedication, that I couldn't say thank you enough.

I also want to thank Rev. David Bonilla. His advice and guidance gave me the push that I needed to start working towards the completion of this text.

Finally, I want to thank Claribel Hernández for translating this book into Spanish. De corazón te doy mil gracias.

Table of Contents

Dedication	ix
Acknowledgements	xi
Foreword	15
Introduction	21

Section 1: Wholeness — 25

    Chapter 1 Are You Ready? — 27

    Chapter 2 Emotional Wholeness — 33

    Chapter 3 God's Timing — 41

Section 2: Personal Development — 47

    Chapter 4 Family Life — 49

    Chapter 5 Be You! — 55

    Chapter 6 Be a Team — 63

Section 3: Spiritual Development — 73

    Chapter 7 Faithful Conduit — 75

    Chapter 8 Have God's Heart — 83

    Chapter 9 Give God Glory — 93

    Chapter 10 Bless and Protect — 99

    Chapter 11 Focus — 107

Section 4: Ministry — 115

    Chapter 12 Leadership Models — 117

    Chapter 13 Equip the Front Line — 125

    Chapter 14 Empower Others — 131

    Chapter 15 Love People — 137

    Chapter 16 Speak Like Jesus — 147

    Chapter 17 The Effective Message — 153

Section 5: Faith — 159

    Chapter 18 Trust & Finances — 161

    Chapter 19 The Anointing — 171

    Chapter 20 Healing Beliefs — 181

    Chapter 21 God of New Things — 191

About the Author — 197

References — 199

Pastor References

Eddie planted in all of us the love for evangelism in our local community and all around the world. He imparted in us the love for foreign missions. (Eddie goes on Mission trips and takes groups from the church with him.) He has also planted in us the love to serve others. Eddie & Martha are the most hospitable people we know. Their home was always open to missionaries, evangelists, other pastors and preachers and to their friends. Many of the young people of that church in Yonkers, NY are now credentialed ministers in the Assemblies of God. Many are Pastors (like we are); others are evangelists. We learned through this couple what true sacrificial love and service really is. We learned that it is all about the people.

Pastors Heriberto and Annie Montalvo

My wife was only 13 years old when Eddie was voted in to be the pastor at our church at that time. She says, that it was through his ministry, that God became so real to her. Her journey into a personal relationship with God began at that very young age. His love for the souls impacted her so, that even today, she carries that same burden for souls. At one of the conventions, one of the members at our church said to my wife "Your style of ministry is very similar to Rev. Rodriguez." He most definitely left his footprint on her life. My wife came from a very dysfunctional family with a lot of challenges. As a pastor, he displayed a shepherd's heart for her family, and was of great support to her mom in many difficult times. For this and more, she is forever grateful.

Pastors Joaquin and Mirta Colon

Foreword

For as long as I can remember, I sat under the covering of a pastor. My father is a minister and held different roles along the years. I was always in the inner circle of the PK kids. As a young adult, I promised myself that I would never marry a pastor. I saw how hard and lonely and challenging it can sometimes get. Since God has a sense of humor, He found a way to lead my husband into that exact calling years after we were married. My husband's spiritual dad is Pastor Eddie.

I learned of Eddie when he became the prodigy pastor within the Assemblies of God. He was the youngest pastor back then, at the tender age of 19. Out of all of the pastors I knew during my youth, Eddie was different. He had the tender heart towards youth like most pastors of the day, but his shift towards how to pastor created a ripple effect of questions. Many asked about his method. His church stood out within the section of Manhattan. He was radical; he was sold out; and he was more interested in God's nod above all others.

When Eddie calls you "pastor" in this book, it's not solely for those who are walking in the fullness of their ministry or have walked this path. It is a prophetic beckoning to step in. To be called has lofty responsibilities, but it also has rewards that far exceed the harsh and lonely times.

This manual took years in the making. God chose Eddie to experience a smorgasbord of real-life struggles, challenges, blessings and miracles, so that he could share many of them with you. When I asked him the why behind this book, he gave me the following Eddie answer without hesitation.

> *"The fuel that compelled me to put my journey on paper was to build a fence at the edge of the cliff, so that we would not have to build a hospital at the bottom of the cliff. I want to prepare the 'Called' to what awaits them. God's dealing with each individual is uniquely-tailored, but the principles are always the same."*

Today, you are reading about his life assignment mixed with sound-counsel from years of experience, and his deep-well of wisdom. You will read about basic principles that should be incorporated, for those who are called, as part of their foundation. His emphasis on the love for souls is throughout this book with the constant reminder that your "do" is always for the glory of God.

You will learn with this manual. You will learn again and again, because part of a shepherd's heart is to grow in the wisdom of servant-leading. It is my expectation that your life will be changed as you turn these pages. I have no doubt that you will gain new perspective and a fresh, new-approach towards pastoring.

You who are called to ministry, you don't arrive on this side of heaven. You journey. Take this manual as part of your journey, and don't be afraid to sail into God's unknown.

~ Roz Humphreys Perez

Introduction

Ministry is for the few, the brave and the called.

I became a Pastor at 19. As I look back, I wished that someone would have coached me and warned me about the minefields and obstacles that could have caused me to abandon ship. As a pastor's son, I looked up to men that had great grace and favor. They had the gift of oratory, with a notable anointing, but were never able to reach their full potential.

I have also seen a troubling trend. There have been many wonderful and good intentioned men and women who have crashed on the rocks of discouragement and despair in their journey. Many started with a clear calling from God to become a pastor with zeal, joy and tenacity. Many embarked in a Bible Institute and college education. Some actually went on to earn their masters and doctorate degrees. When they entered into the ministry, wide-eyed and filled with Godly dreams and desires, they were filled with potential. Yet, the pressures of ministry began to wear them down. One by one, I witnessed certain individuals get weary and tired. They faltered and failed to fulfill their potential. Many have hung up their priestly robes, never to put them back on again, as published in Pastoral Care Inc.

Each month, 1700 pastors quit the ministry; one of 10 will

actually retire from the ministry in some form; and 50% of pastors want to leave the ministry because they are so discouraged, but can't because they have no other way of making a living.

This field manual is for those who have been called to ministry. This is for both the emerging leaders that initially responded to God's call to "love and feed His sheep," as well as those with years of ministry, who have battle scars of experience and desire encouragement and inspiration.

My writing will be based on my journey and ministry. It covers many aspects of pastoral responsibilities and expectations. I have had the privilege of being in the Pastoral and Evangelistic ministries. I have had the privilege of starting five churches, and pastoring three that have grown exponentially. As an evangelist, I have gone the breadth and length of the United States, and have visited most of Latin America, Europe, Africa and the Far East. I have seen thousands respond to the Holy Spirit, and surrender their lives to the Savior. I have made many mistakes, and I have learned from them. My hope is that this manual will keep you from making the same mistakes, and inspire you to greater heights in your ministry.

As you set off on this wonderful journey, I would like to encourage you to take this field manual with you. My prayer is that every person that reads this book will be encouraged and inspired to fulfill their full-potential, with joy and excellence.

Note:

Throughout these pages, you will see the phrase "The Holy Spirit told me." Whenever you read this, it is not an audible voice. It is an impressive clarity in my understanding, or sudden conviction and perception that comes without expectation. It is that moment that is birthed by the Holy Spirit.

When God calls you to something, He is not always calling you to succeed; He's calling you to obey! The success of the calling is up to Him; the obedience is up to you.
David Wilkerson

**God's will is your success...
so learn to be obedient!**

Section 1
Wholeness

Chapter 1
Are You Ready?

*God doesn't call the equipped.
He equips the called!*
AUTHOR UNKNOWN

You feel called!
Does this mean that you are ready?

The driving force that should be behind your calling is passion for the lost and great love for God and His church. It is one thing to be handed a letter of recruitment, and it is another thing to be handed a notice of deployment. Many rush into their calling prematurely. In reality, you will never feel completely sufficient, and you won't ever feel quite ready when it comes to being a pastor or any leader in the kingdom of God. We know that God equips and uses those that feel the most unworthy. He does this so that you may always know that He gets all the glory. This does not excuse you from striving to give God your best.

You can have natural abilities, but you must make them better.

For example, you may have an ear for music and the ability

to play an instrument, but if you do not practice, you will limit your gift. Those that have the gift and go to school and practice, excel above the rest. And so it is with ministry.

Education

What are the things that you need to develop? You could start with your vocabulary. Remember, you have been called to express the ineffable. How can you do that if you cannot express yourself? Education is a necessary tool in ministry. If you cannot go to a formal school, read, read and read some more. Choose books that will stretch your vocabulary and intellect. This does not mean that you should use big words because that will turn off most of your audience. However, education will give you the ability to be concise and clear in your delivery.

Serve

1. Find a mentor and be faithful and loyal.
2. Serve in your local church faithfully.

Learn how to be a loyal servant. You will reap what you sow. The word speaks of this dynamic, "If you are faithful in the small things you will be given bigger responsibilities."

Matthew 25:23.

Observe David's heart. He served Saul and never went against him. Although he had many reasons to rebel against Saul, he stayed faithful. We see other examples in Scripture where others were not as patient and things did not turn out so well. God will fulfill His purpose for you in due time. All He asks of you is to be faithful and loyal where you are, and to wait on Him. He doesn't need your help to fulfill his will in your life.

You will learn many things when you become a diligent servant in the church. You will see inspiring characteristics but also some that are not so inspiring. You will learn how to do things and how not to do things. You might even help a ministry that may not necessarily be what God is preparing you for. Remember, there are stages in your life. Know when one ends and another begins.

Learn to be Obedient

You must learn how to listen to the Holy Spirit, and be obedient to His leading.

One of the many ways that God taught me this lesson was in giving. As a 23-year-old Pastor, I received approximately $7000 to disperse in Haiti and in the Dominican Republic. In the 70s, I had no credit cards or checks. I actually stuffed my wallet, pockets and socks with $20 bills. I felt a great responsibility on my shoulders. As I traveled, the Holy Spirit would give me the green light to give the money away and would stop me when it wasn't His will. I encountered many people I wanted to bless, but God wouldn't let me. On the last day, I had a specific amount left to give. No matter how hard I tried, the Holy Spirit would not give me the permission to release the money. I started to ask the Lord why? I didn't want to take this money back to the States. My brother-in-law and I decided to visit a girl's orphanage in Port-au-Prince. When we walked in, we noticed that the director of the orphanage was crying. The government had begun to confiscate all the furniture because of a debt that they owed. I asked her what the amount of the debt was. It was the exact amount that I had left. The Holy Spirit gave me the green light to pay that debt. If I had not obeyed His leading, I would have not had the money necessary to pay off this debt.

I learned a very important lesson. Don't be led by what you see or feel. Learn how to discern the voice of the Holy Spirit.

Remember Paul? He was on his way to Asia because he saw a need, but the Holy Spirit sent him to Macedonia. This is of upmost importance as a shepherd in God's kingdom, because if you do not know how to listen to the Holy Spirit, you can lead people to step out of the will of God. In a later chapter I will elaborate more on the importance of obedience.

Learn the Bible

"...Out of the abundance of the heart, the mouth speaks." (Luke 6:45)

From this verse, we learn that in order to know someone, you must listen to them speak. So in order to know God's heart, you must listen to him speak, through His word. The Bible is God's word. You have to learn God's word so that you can discern His heart. I will never forget how the Holy Spirit nudged me to go to Bible school. I was a 15-year-old evangelist and I was a pastor's son. I was raised in church, went to Sunday school and my dad read the Bible to us every night. I felt like I didn't need to go to Bible school. One night, I was in an all-night prayer service. At about 2 a.m., something inside of me began to ask, "Who is Hosea?" What were the circumstances in which the Minor Prophets spoke? The questions asked were met with silence. At that moment, I realized how biblically illiterate I was. Also during that time, a person that did not share my beliefs confronted me. He challenged me to prove the deity of Christ, the rapture and many more of my core beliefs, and he wanted Scriptures. I made a decision to study this book called the Bible. It has been my life's passion to be an excellent Bible expositor. I began to ask God in prayer to grant me a doctorate in the Bible.

In this season of preparation, you will also serve in many aspects. You might even enter a ministry. It is of utmost important that you remain in a state of learning and growing. Keep in mind that sometimes what God prepares you for is far in the future, and every step is a molding process.

Enjoy the present. The future will come in due time. This other point of preparation leads me to the next chapter; Emotional Health.

Are You Ready?

What are your thoughts about this chapter? What stood out? What areas need to change?

Chapter 2
Emotional Wholeness

*The church is not made up of spiritual giants;
Only broken men can lead others to the cross.*
DAVID J. BOSCH

Hurting shepherds hurt sheep.
Healed wounds create anointing.

I knew a young pastor that started in ministry with open wounds. Since childhood, his father would compare him to his big brother. He was constantly telling him that he wasn't as smart, and also told him that he would not amount to anything in life. He carried this opened wound into the pastorate. As a matter of fact, he would lash out when anyone disagreed with him. He would feel that if anyone did not agree with his ideas or gave a different opinion that they were against him. He fired the board and surrounded himself with yes men. His constant tongue lashing towards those that dared to question his decisions caused many to leave his church, and eventually, he left the pastorate. This also caused him to lose credibility as a spiritual leader and projected a tarnished image of Christ. The pressure of being a pastor was too great for him. This so-called pressure was self-made. These wounds that festered in his soul stunted God's best for him.

Bitterness

Bitterness is the only sin that the bible tacked on the word "root." (Hebrews 12:15)

It's called the root of bitterness because, just like the roots of a tree, it will grow into every corner of your life. It affects the way you treat your family and in your everyday relationships. Festered wounds cause you to lash out at people without warning, much like a hunted prey that is suddenly devoured when they least expected. You will lash out at people without control, if you harbor bitterness. It may cause you to withdraw at the slightest perception of being attacked. In ministry, you need to make sure that those wounds are healed. The only things that should remain are scars which are the proof of healing.

How can you get healed?

I am glad you asked. The first step is to recognize that you have been wounded, and that it is humanly impossible for it to heal by itself. Sin, especially the root of bitterness, is unnatural to humans. God created us in His image and likeness. When sin crept into our souls, we were defenseless. I compare this to the Everglades in Florida. People are destroying the Everglades by abandoning animals and planting vegetation that are not natural to the ecosystem. As a result, these unnatural visitors are growing without hindrance because they have no natural predators to keep them in check. They are killing the natural plants and animals. So it is with sin, and the root of bitterness. We have no natural defenses in our lives against these intruders, especially with wounds that were caused by adults that were considered protectors during childhood. Sexual and verbal abuse suffered at childhood is unbelievably destructive.

Four-Throng Approach

Here is a four-throng approach to fight the Root of Bitterness.

1. **Recognize that you are wounded**. You cannot heal if you do not identify the wounds. Ignoring these issues will cause these wounds to grow without restraints.

2. **Pray over it**. Confess it to the Lord. Ask Him to forgive you for holding on to bitterness.

3. **Forgive those that wounded you**. This might be one of the most difficult ones to do. You must forgive as God has forgiven you. This might have to be done in faith. Confess that you forgive them and pray for them. God's grace will enable you to overcome this hurdle. If the person that wounded you is still alive, call them and tell them that you forgive them. In some situations, you have to forgive daily in your prayers. Sometimes people continue to hurt you, or

the memories keep coming back. You must be in a constant state of forgiveness.

4. **Bring it to light**. Talk about it with others. This is very effective because it will no longer be a secret, dark and foreboding area in your life. When something like this is suppressed, it just festers. When you shine the light on your struggles, it weakens their hold on you. I compare sin to a cockroach. These nasty critters come out when the lights are turned off. When the lights are switched on, they run. You must decide if you need biblical or professional counseling. This will depend on your healing process. If you don't forgive, you become what you hate. You will, most likely, imitate the person you won't forgive

Emotional Preparation

Many people enter the ministry with intellectual preparation, but no emotional preparation.

When I served as an executive officer in my denomination, I observed that the pastors were the cause of many church conflicts. When you enter the ministry you are called to be a participant with the Holy Spirit to build people. You will be faced with great challenges. People that are hurt will lash out at you, malign you and criticize everything you do. They will comment on the way you dress, talk and walk. Some will criticize your new car, and some will criticize even when you have an old car. Some will love your preaching, and some will say that they were not fed, and that your message did not edify them. They will scream at you and verbally abuse your family. Some will go against giving you a raise and will say that they have more pressing needs than your salary.

As young pastors, my wife and I experienced this. We started to pastor at the ages of 18 and 19. We were ill-prepared for what was to come. As newlyweds do, we began to gain weight. People started to say, "Those pastors obviously don't fast." We started to exercise and watch our food intake and lost weight. Then we began to hear "They got skinny because of their failed business dealings." We were also financially strapped, so my wife would wear the same clothes. We then heard "That pastor's wife always wears the same clothes." When God blessed us and we started to dress better, we heard "Those pastors spend the church's money in clothes." Looking back I laugh, but at that moment, it was hurtful.

When I would purchase something for the church, someone always commented that I paid too much for it and that I was wasting church money. One year the church decided to buy me a new car. I got a phone call from a member who asked if he could borrow my car. I knew he had a car so I told him that I would lend him my car, but asked why he needed my car. His answer was "I want to teach my wife how to drive, and I don't want to risk her crashing my car."

These are just a few incidents that I've been through in ministry. When I started, these were hurtful because I wasn't forewarned. Now I truly laugh when I hear this.

I'm painting this dark picture to ask you this one question. Are you emotionally equipped to answer with love and not get defensive and bitter?

Maybe one day, the ones you spend more time with and consider your friends, will let you know that they're leaving to another church. How will you handle this? You will need to bless them and thank them for their years of service. You will need to not speak ill of them or cut them off. Speak blessings upon them. We are called to reflect Jesus to those we serve (1 Corinthians 11:1). Are you emotionally ready? Are you emotionally mature enough to react in love and compassion? Or, will you feel offended, rejected and start speaking against people that have hurt you or left your church?

Many times, people have entered into ministry with emotional wounds. They had wounds that have been with them since childhood and these wounds dictate their mood and actions. Some of us were constantly put down, and grew up in very dysfunctional families. These unresolved wounds, will control actions and cause one to lash out or fall into depression. Instead of giving a loving and edifying response to wounded people, they choose to enter into conflict and cause bigger wounds.

The shepherd must always respond in love. Bless those that hurt you. Bless those that leave your church. As you go forth in the midst of opposition, abide in it with joy and compassion. Always remember, Jesus loves them and died for them. This is one of the lessons Christ taught the disciples when He admonished them to deny themselves and take up their cross daily (Luke 9:23). This means that you must put aside your desires, to fulfill His, and to have the heart of God.

The good news is that healed wounds become scars of experience. (Luke 22:31-32)

These scars will release an anointing to be a blessing to others. Scarred soldiers tell the tale. You know they've been in battle and survived. When you look upon the scars of a soldier, you feel grateful and inspired. Use your healed wounds as testimonies of God's grace. You cannot minister effectively with open wounds. They will fester, and if left unattended, will eventually require amputation or cause death.

I will not get into the psychological baggage we can carry, but I will say this, seek help. You may need to talk to a counselor and deal with your wounds. If not, as I stated earlier, it will stunt the growth of your ministry, and will affect your family and even your marriage.

As you go forth into fulfilling your calling, you need to keep in mind this process. Sometimes while going through emotional healing, God will nudge you to go forward. As long as you recognize this healing process and submit to it, God will lead you to a greater degree of maturity.

The question that then arises is, "How do I know when it is God's time for me?" Let's address this in the following chapter. It will help you understand God's timing.

What are your thoughts about this chapter? What stood out? What areas need to change?

_____

_____

_____

_____

_____

_____

_____

_____

_____

_____

Chapter 3
God's Timing

Great leader's courage to fulfill his vision comes from passion, not position.
JOHN MAXWELL

God will open the doors in His timing, and scripture is filled with examples of God's timing.

There is a season for all things.

Your life will have seasons according to God's plan for you. You must be patient and learn how to wait on God. When it's God's time to move you, he will open the right doors. He will put the right people in your path. The Bible says, be anxious for nothing (Philippians 4:8). Many ministers fail, not because God did not call them, but because they did not wait for God's timing. They proceeded prematurely. If you walk side-by-side with Jesus, you will see the doors of opportunities open. Don't walk in front of Him, or behind him; but walk beside Him. He will gently guide you into your destiny and His purpose.

He will not force you to walk beside him in obedience. You have free will and can choose to do things your way. But if you humbly walk His way, deny yourself and take up your cross, you will see things that you cannot imagine. For this, you need to be patient and let Him show you His glory in His timing.

When God's timing arrives for your ministry it will be beyond what you expected. (Ephesians 3:20)

I hear many young preachers complain that no one gives them an opportunity to preach. I cannot understand that gripe. If you are truly called by God to be a minister you start to minister. You don't wait for a pulpit to minister. Compassion is what causes you to minister on street corners, hospitals and to your neighbors. As a 15 year old, filled with love and a desire to win souls for Christ, I proclaimed Christ on the street corners of New York City. Many weekends, I traveled from 42nd street in Manhattan to 168th street. I would stop every two blocks and preach the gospel. I would make a calling and prayed for the sick. At 16, I went to the Dominican Republic and ministered in public places. I would even go to small, remote villages on horseback and preach the gospel. I was not interested in preaching in a church. The lost were outside the church. Pastors would observe me preaching on street corners and then would invite me to their churches. Sometimes I would accept the invitations, grudgingly.

The gifts of the Holy Spirit always move mightily when you go to the un-churched. That's why they are given, so that the church can wage war against the enemy and rescue the lost. As I focused on preaching to the lost, I experienced God opening other doors.

The first door that opened for me was to become pastor of a Spanish church in New York named "Filipo's Church." At 19, my Spanish was very limited. While pastoring, God also opened doors for crusades throughout Latin America.

One day, when I was in a restaurant having lunch with my dad, a stranger walked up to me and asked if I was a preacher. He introduced himself as a pastor in South America that coordinated crusades for Billy Graham. He offered to coordinate crusades for me in South America. He had never heard me preach nor did he know me. God's timing is perfect. He went on to organize massive crusades, and I saw the glory of God like never before. Thousands came to the Lord during those crusades. God opened that door. I had nothing to do with it. He did it all. God's favor will open doors in His time.

We were scheduled to go through Virginia in one of my evangelistic trips with my family. I have always wanted to visit John Giménez' church, so we went to his Sunday morning service. We arrived early but still ended up in the balcony, all the way in the last seats. As he was preaching, he would look up at me. When the service finished, he pointed at me and called me to him. We found our way to the front and he hugged me and said,

"Who are you that I feel so much love for you?" That began a relationship that opened many doors.

Again God's favor will open the doors in His time. The Bible says that in the last days God has opened a door that no man can shut. (Revelation 3:8)

Go forth with confidence.

Preach this glorious gospel. Lift up Christ and always remember; it is Him doing everything. It is about Him. To Him belongs all the Glory.

Also, always remember, after having done all, bow before Him and say "Unworthy servant am I; I have only done what has been demanded of me (Luke 17:10).

What are your thoughts about this chapter? What stood out? What areas need to change?

Section 2
Personal Development

Chapter 4
Family Life

*You don't choose your family.
They are God's gift to you, as you are to them.*
DESMOND TUTU

Your Spouse

The biggest let down is when you realize that your spouse cannot totally fill that void. Adam was created first. His joy and comfort was in his creator. Once he learned to live alone, then God created in him the desire for a companion (Genesis 2:18-21). We must come to the realization that God and only God will be fully sufficient. Then, we will be ready to create a happy home. The moral, emotional and spiritual support of your spouse will determine your joy in ministry. Being a leader can create social loneliness. Your spouse should be your best friend, your confidante and the shoulder you cry on. You should protect your spouse by giving them the place they deserve, with your time and your attentiveness.

Always speak of your spouse from your pulpit. Let your congregation know how in love you are. This will dispense adulteress thoughts from the mind of someone under your ministry. Also, a leader will always have people that will feel unwarranted-attraction towards them. Therefore, a healthy marriage is of utmost importance in the ministry. A healthy marriage will protect you from unhealthy relationships with the opposite sex. For this reason, you must dedicate time and energy towards your marriage. The ministry can put a lot of pressure on your family. It depends on you to alleviate this pressure and make ministry a joy for your home.

Have a Healthy Sex Life

Many enter into marriage thinking that sex is dirty and sinful. As a leader in my denomination, I have seen marriages and ministries destroyed because of an unhealthy attitude towards intimacy in marriage. It's worse if you were raised in a church that only talks about sex in the context of sin. Your conscience becomes damaged. You cannot enjoy sex with your spouse without feeling dirty and sinful. And, after having sex, you ask God for forgiveness. If any or all of the above happens in your marriage bed, you are heading for disaster. This is something that you need to address. It will not go away. It will only get worse if you ignore it. The only things that will go away if you ignore them are your teeth.

The number one target of Satan is your marriage. If you are not married yet, have pre-marital counseling with someone that will address this issue with confidence and boldness.

The apostle Paul said that if you deny each other sex, Satan will take advantage and will slither into your marriage (Corinthians 7:5). The Holy text commands, *"Don't deny your spouse." "Your body is not your own."* 1 Corinthians 7:4. Marriage is a surrendering one to another. It clearly states that if you have a need for sex, get married (1 Corinthians 7:2). It doesn't say to pray and it will go away. No, it says to enjoy it with your spouse. Intimacy and sex is a physical and emotional need. To say that if you pray it will go away is like saying "If your spouse doesn't feed you, just pray and fast. Don't worry about eating. Prayer will take care of it, **"NO!"** If you have this situation, please take it seriously and work on fixing it. Sometimes couples feel embarrassed to talk about this. This shouldn't stop you from doing what's necessary to make your marriage a happy one. A pastor with a healthy marriage is a happy pastor and an effective leader. This will allow you to be transparent.

You must separate yourself from your church once you are home. Live a normal life. Don't talk of church problems at home. Play games, share jokes, go out for dinner. Have a date night. Take at least one day a week and dedicate it to your family. Turn off the cell phone and do things together that are not related to ministry. Take vacations. (Going to conventions and conferences is not a vacation.) If you have children, take two separate vacations. Take one with the kids and the other just with your spouse. You will be surprised at the results. I have fallen in love with my wife over and over again in these "parents only" vacations.

Children

Don't forget to be a pastor to your children.

We forget that the kids in our church have this role separately. They have parents, and they have a pastor. Our children have both parent and pastor in one.

One day I was called to speak to the guidance counselor of one of my children. They told me how they were behaving in a disrespectful and disruptive manner. I was shocked and angered. I walked my grown (approximately 15 year old) child to my car and started to head home. Then the thought came to me. "Your child needs a pastor right now, not a father." I turned the car towards the church. We entered my office and I counseled my child as her pastor not as an angry and embarrassed dad. It was awesome. That child opened her heart and accepted Christ that day.

In my travels I have seen many denominations and church boards displace a pastor because their children have strayed away from the Lord.

They used the scripture that says that a leader in the church should have their family under submission. Many have abused this verse. It refers to minor children. Once they become adults, they are no longer under the parents. Salvation is not inherited. Even if you are born into a Christian family, this does not make you a Christian. Children have to be born again and have their personal experience. To say that the father has not done a good job, because of a backslidden adult child, is totally incorrect. If this were true, then God failed when **His** son, Adam, backslid. Also the father of the prodigal son (which is a symbol of our Heavenly Father) did a lousy job as a father. If for these foolish reasons you are displaced of a pastorate, just continue your ministry elsewhere. Don't allow anyone to strip you of your calling. *The gifts and calling of God are irrevocable.* Romans 11:29

Your home should be your "happy place." It should be the place that gives you comfort, peace and rest. Do not take problems to your home. Having a healthy family is imperative for the enjoyment of your life and ministry. As a garden, your family requires constant care. As a minister of the gospel, you should also feel free to seek help and counseling when needed. Work your marriage and do not allow problems to fester.

Remember, you and your family are also sheep, and you need to go seek help just like your congregants. Do not fall into the trap of "keeping appearances." The desire to appear as someone you are not, will cause great damage to your spouse and children, and will also rob you of God's best for you. Let's talk about this in the next chapter.

Family Life

What are your thoughts about this chapter? What stood out? What areas need to change?

_____

_____

_____

_____

_____

_____

_____

_____

_____

_____

_____

Chapter 5
Be You!

*Jesus called fishermen, not graduates of rabbinical schools.
The main requirement to serve the Lord
was to be natural and sincere!*
JIM CYMBALA

Be yourself, everybody else is already taken.
OSCAR WILDE

You must be who God made you to be and not the old Adam.

Your sinful nature must be done away with. That sinful nature is a reflection of the father of sin, Satan. You must be the new Adam.

> *"Wherein ye also once walked, when ye lived in these things; lie not one to another; seeing that ye have put off the old man with his doings, and have put on the new man, that is being renewed unto knowledge after the image of him that created him:"*
> Colossians 3:7, 9-10 (ASV)

The born again person that reflect the likeness and image of our Heavenly Father. They have a redeemed spirit that now has a Godly fruit. It is that renewed spirit in every human being, that when quickened by the Holy Spirit through his word, springs Godly characteristics (Galatians 5). This new birth does not take away your uniqueness. Every one of us was created with different gifts and abilities. Before, they were used for selfish and worldly pleasures. Now they are used for God's kingdom. It takes time to develop and/or discover who you are. As you grow in grace, it will become more definable. Some will like you and some won't, but that's all right, you can't please everybody. If you try to please everyone you will be a miserable pastor.

As a young minister, I heard countless times, this saying. "The pastor has to be like that clown that was sad but always put on a smile." This advice almost cost me my ministry. I was being told not to let people see my pain and conflicts. To hide who I am. As a result of this advice, I did not confide with anyone about my problems. When they surfaced, it was too late. The destruction was devastating, but it was a blessing in disguise. I finally was able to confront what was hindering my happiness.

Take Off the Veil

Using the law of double reference, I'm reminded of the scripture that commands us to take away the mask (2 Corinthians 3:16). I remember when I was offered to submit my candidacy for a small church in Yonkers, New York. The church was so small, that it didn't even have enough money to offer a salary. I was still in Bible School, and was not doing much, so they asked me if I was willing to help out. My wife was not too happy about this. She never wanted to be a pastor's wife. I had been evangelizing since I was 15 and she was happy with me being an evangelist. We had just gotten married and she was pregnant with our first child. I finally got her to agree that it would be just until God would lead us elsewhere. In our first meeting with the deacons, they expressed their concerns. Their first advice was that we should not be seen talking to the youth, because we were too young and the older folks might not like that. Their second advice was for us to dress older. Well the first week that I preached, my wife put her hair up into two ponytails and wore tennis shoes. Nevertheless, we were voted in and pastored there for 10 years. The church grew powerfully and within a year, we bought a supermarket and converted it into a church building. The presence of God was ever-present, but I hid who I really was. I had to pretend that I was older and very serious. Those that knew me well knew that I was not like that. For 10 years I pretended to be this serious, older guy. I was not happy. I saw God's hand move mightily and many came to Christ, but I felt totally unfulfilled.

I left in 1981 to full-time evangelism. When the Lord started nudging me to start a church in West Palm Beach, FL, I had a heart-to-heart conversation with my Lord. I shared with Him that I will pastor again if I could be me. I didn't want to hide who I truly was. I would not pretend to be someone I'm not. Little did I know that I was entering into my anointing and favor. I became the happiest pastor on earth. God's anointing and favor was increased immensely.

We must understand that God has made you and there is no one else like you.

God has given you a unique favor and grace.

> *"But unto each one of us was the grace given according to the measure of the gift of Christ."*
> Ephesians 4:7 (ASV)

> *"But we will not glory beyond our measure, but according to the measure of the province which God apportioned to us as a measure, to reach even unto you."*
> 2 Corinthians 10:13 (ASV)

You must let your God-given talents and gifts shine. You don't have to imitate another preacher or project someone you're not.

> "For we are not bold to number or compare ourselves with certain of them that commend themselves: but they themselves, measuring themselves by themselves, and comparing themselves with themselves, are without understanding."   2 Corinthians 10:12 (ASV)
> *"But let each man prove his own work, and then*

shall he have his glorying in regard of himself alone, and not of his neighbor."
Galatians 6:4 (ASV)

As I said earlier, not everyone will like you, but that's all right. Many will be drawn to your style of ministry. You have a unique ministry that's needed in the kingdom of God.

Let people see you as you are. Sometimes we think that we need to project perfection to inspire others. I've realized that instead of inspiring others they get discouraged.

When they see that God uses you in spite of and not because of you, they then start walking in HIS grace and feel that God can use them too. You will be happier in your ministry and your family will also enjoy your journey.

My children did not have the pressure of having to be perfect.

They were able to walk in their reality. Whenever someone would try to correct them just because they were the pastor's kids, I would stop them and not allow that type of correction. I would tell them to correct them as if they were just another kid in church, nothing more...nothing less.

If you have to hide who you are, work on your integrity and put it in prayer before the Lord. Get counseling and become whole in your personality. In your transparency, the Lord's grace and mercy shall follow you all the days of your life. Your message will be fresh and relevant, and you will be free of other's opinions. Integrity means that you are of one piece. You are the same person with others at work, home or with a friend. You do not have multiple faces.

Eddie Rodriguez

What are your thoughts about this chapter? What stood out? What areas need to change?

Chapter 6
Be a Team

*The role of a pastor is not to grow a big church.
The pastor's role is to grow
mature disciples who make disciple.*
RICK HOWERTON

*The strength of the team is each individual member.
The strength of each member is the team.*
PHIL JACKSON

Jesus sent them two by two. He always walked with His disciples. He worked with a team.

We need to do the same. Not only will this give us great synergy, but it will also create true disciples. The word says one will put a thousand to flight and two shall put 10,000 to flight (Deuteronomy 32:30).

True discipleship is walking with that person. It's not only about preaching and giving a Bible class. The Bible instructs the members to consider their pastor's behavior and imitate their conduct. They can't imitate your talents (Hebrew 13:17). Discipleship is befriending people and letting them into your inner circle. It's applying the scriptures to their experiences in a practical context (Deuteronomy 6:7) and in turn, teaching each member to do the same.

Scriptures clearly teaches the importance of multiplication.

God gives utmost importance to numbers. So much so, that there is a book in the Bible called "Numbers." It is God's will for his Kingdom and His word to fill the earth as waters cover the sea.

You Cannot Do It by Yourself

Years ago, I was listening to a preacher speak in a youth rally. I was 15 and had just started wanting more of God in my life. He spoke about having the hand of God upon you, and how men in the Bible did mighty exploits because of God's hand upon them. I got so hungry for God's hand to be in my life that I went home and told my mother that I would spend that night in prayer. I grabbed a blanket and locked myself in the bathroom and started calling out to God, asking Him to place His hand on my head. I was so hungry and desperate for God that I did not try to understand what it was that I was expecting. All I know is that God's presence filled the room with awesome glory. I shook like a tree hammered by a mighty wind, but I said, "No God that's not what I'm asking for. I want your hand on my head." I prayed until daylight was about to break. I didn't change my prayer. I pleaded incessantly for His hand to be placed on my head. All of the sudden, I saw myself in a great expanse, surrounded by a blue sky. There appeared a cloud, and out of that cloud a beam shot down and struck me on my head. At that moment I received an unexpected conviction. I cried out to God and asked that He would rise up laborers, prophets, preachers, and evangelist. I felt so insufficient before the great need and the vast task beforehand. I felt something that has been with me throughout my ministry. I have learned the importance of working as a team, to create disciples and to desire His best for other ministers.

We must learn to work as a team with the local pastors in our city.

A true revival will only come when we realize that although there are many congregations in one city, there is only one church. This church must come together and work towards the common goal, that none should perish but that all should come to repentance. True growth in God's kingdom is not having your church grow by members changing churches. It grows when people come to a saving knowledge of Christ. Angels rejoice, not when a member changes to another congregation, but when someone accepts Christ as their Lord and Savior.

It's a blessing to have a team.

Whether they are called Deacons or Elders, we as pastors of the flock, must have counselors and people we should count on. First let's define what is a Deacon and an Elder. The

Bible clearly states that Deacons were chosen to ***"Serve the Tables"*** (Acts 6:1-6). In today's church, it would be to do the administrative work in the church. Their job releases the pastors so that they can invest their time in prayer and the word. Isn't that awesome? We get paid to pray and study God's word. What a privilege we have. When the Deacons do their part it frees the pastor to be in "the mountain," to intercede for his sheep and ask for a word from heaven to relay to the congregation. The Deacons should tend to all things that are necessary for a church to run smoothly; from making sure the building is clean and ready for service; to paying the bills and tending to the social needs of the community; or feeding the hungry and washing the dishes. They need to be the ones that roll up their sleeves and do what's necessary to keep things in order. And, to do this, they must first have to be filled with the Holy Spirit and fulfill all the requirements in the scriptures given for this office (I Timothy 3:8-13).

Many pastors have assigned people to serve in this office solely based on their business acumen or because they have experience in finances. While this is a good thing, above all these attributes, they must be spiritual people with a good reputation and men and women of vision. Many churches have been destroyed by having carnal Deacons that are not sensitive towards others and in-tune with the Holy Spirit.

Many confuse the line between Deacons and Elders to their peril.

A board of Elders should be your pastoral staff; all those that minister along with the pastor.

The Associate Pastors should be considered the Elders of the church (Acts 20:28). With them, you consult spiritual matters and sensitive situations that might merit consultation.

I've learned that both boards are placed to be a blessing to the Pastor.

The Bible says that in the multitude of counsel, there is wisdom (Proverbs 15:22). It also clearly teaches that we must submit one to another. They are there to protect you and walk alongside you, to give advice and to seek God's will for the church with you. They should not be yes men. They should be free to give different perspectives and opinions. They should feel free to disagree without being obstinate; all submitting, one to another. They should seek God's mind for the church.

As a young pastor starting in the ministry, I learned a valuable lesson. When I wanted to do something, and there wasn't an agreement within my leaders, it was always God protecting me. I learned through trial and error that they were a blessing placed there by God to help me do the right thing. I've learned that this is God's kingdom. He is in control of His kingdom. It is not my role to fight or have an antagonistic relationship with my board. I must submit to them as they also must submit to me. We must obey the scriptures and submit one to another (Ephesians 5:21). If disagreements arise, be silent and let God handle it.

One day I was in prayer and I had a strong conviction that I had to preach in a crusade in Mexico. I told my wife what I felt that the Holy Spirit was telling me. In less than an hour, I got a call from a pastor in Mexico asking me to hold a crusade in his city. I immediately agreed because of what the Holy Spirit impressed on me earlier. The next day I called a meeting with my Elders and Deacons and shared with them about the call I got from Mexico. I did not tell them of my experience in prayer. I have always been cautious not to say "God told me" because I believed that this could lead to manipulation. If it is truly God, He will bring it to pass without having to sell the idea. The Head Deacon stood up and spoke against it. He mentioned the fact that we were under persecution. The church building had been closed by the city, and we did not know where our next service would be. How could I leave now, when the church most needed me? He convinced the whole board not to let me go to give the crusade. I also agreed with their decision. It made sense. We adjourned the meeting with the decision that I couldn't go to hold the crusade in Mexico.

I wasn't concerned at all. You see, God is a God of order. His word clearly teaches that we must submit one to the other. He would never want me to argue or quarrel with my Deacons and Elders, so I just went to God in prayer. I told the Lord what He already knew. "You told me to go but you also say in your word to submit. This is your fight. I put this in your hands." I went to sleep with not a care in the world. Pastor, this is God's work. He will move whatever He needs to move. It didn't end there. The next morning, at 7 a.m., my phone rang. I picked up the phone and someone was crying on the other end. It was the Head Deacon. He had a dream. In that dream, he saw thousands of souls falling in a bottomless pit. He looked up and saw our Lord Jesus Christ, and with love and tenderness told him, "Thousands will go to hell because you will not let my servant go." He called a meeting with all the Deacons and the Elders and shared his dream. They all agreed that I must go. They even collected an offering for my trip. God is in control.

Your job is to love and be an example of tenderness and respect.

My number one rule for my entire staff, both paid and volunteer is to never be abrasive or offensive. They are always to respond in love and tenderness. If they cannot, they should not be in leadership positions in God's kingdom. Why? The truth is that it is all about loving and building people. It's about showing what Jesus is all about with your conduct.

Please pastor, walk in peace. The Lord will fight your battles. Your job is to care for those that God has put before you, and to do it with joy.

To have a healthy church you must have a pastoral team.

A church that expects the senior pastor to be in every meeting and in every service is a dysfunctional church. The senior pastor will quickly suffer burnout, and his family will become bitter. You must absent yourself intentionally and delegate too. Trust those you delegate. You must have your function in this battle clearly defined.

I can do things you cannot.
You can do things I cannot.
Together we can do great things.
MOTHER TERESA

Eddie Rodriguez

What are your thoughts about this chapter? What stood out? What areas need to change?

Section 3
Spiritual Development

Chapter 7
Faithful Conduit

Not only must the message be correctly delivered, but the messenger himself must be such as to recommend it to acceptance.
JOSEPH BARBER LIGHTFOOT

When I first saw the girl that was to be my wife, I was only 13 and she was 12. I was the pastor's son and her mom told her that she should go to church to meet the pastor's son. When I saw her, I told my older brother that she was going to be my wife. She struck my heart, but I was very shy and didn't dare approach her. So, one day I asked a friend of mine to ask her to be my girlfriend. He went to talk to her and when he came back, he said, "she said no". Well I was glad she told him and not me, but during the service, we kept looking at each other. About a week later, I asked my friend to ask her again. He once again told me that she said no. I was confused because she continued to look at me. So, after some weeks, I gathered enough courage to approach her. I asked her why she was rejecting me. To my surprise, she said that she had said yes from the start. My "friend" was also interested in her and would change the message.

How many times has that happened to our loving Lord? Many preachers change the message.

We preach and reflect a tarnished image of who he really is. Our main goal should be to be faithful messengers and not rewrite the letter. Just deliver it intact (Hebrew 1:1-3).

In order to do this, you must die to self.

Our pride and our fears should not stand in the way of God's message. You must speak in such a way that Christ is exalted and not you. You must do His works and will, without fearing the opinions of others. The fear of men should not dictate your ministry.

One day, I invited a preacher to come and minister. I had never seen God use someone like that. He would minister over the sick, and if they would not get healed, he would minister through the gift of knowledge. He would minister to their hearts and pray for healing again, and Jesus would heal them. I had Holy envy. After the service, I asked my wife to go home because I wanted to talk to this preacher. I grabbed him by the arm and sat him in my car. I looked at him and said, "Why does God use you so much. Please don't tell me that it's because you fast and pray. I know a lot of people that fast and pray, and they are not used as much. I was surprised by his answer. He said, "The day I lost my fear of the opinions of others was when I allowed the Holy Spirit to use me."

Be a Faithful Conduit

In 1976, I went to Chile in South America to hold four major crusades. I was hungry to see God move with his healing power. I would lock myself in the hotel where I was staying at and spent hours in prayer. I called unto God, and asked Him many questions. I reminded Him of what Jesus said, how we would do greater things than He; of how He went to many cities; and how He healed all of the sick. I inquired as to why we haven't seen that in our ministries. Then I thought... maybe it's because He was God, but then I remembered that He said that He did it by the power of the Holy Spirit. He told the people words like "According to your faith it will be done" and "Your faith has made you whole." As I meditated on this, the following passage in Romans came to me. "Faith comes by hearing the word of God." Right then, I understood that people received miracles because Christ spoke in such a way that all who heard Him received faith for their miracle.

Paul asked for prayer that he might speak with boldness and clarity. I began to plead in prayer that I might speak as Jesus spoke, and that my flesh, or my thoughts would not hinder His word. I wanted His words to flow from me to others with clarity and boldness. I asked that the unadulterated and undiluted word may flow from my lips. That night, I stood before the multitude that was gathered in a sports stadium in Chile, and opened my mouth. I had, what seemed to me, like an outer-body experience. The words that were coming out of my mouth were much bigger than me. I remember listening to myself and saying "Eddie what are you doing? If nothing happens tonight you are going to be run out of this town as a false prophet. Look at all these news reporters sitting in the front."

When I finished preaching, I felt naked and afraid. I turned around and gave the microphone to the nearest pastor. I didn't dare make an altar call. I knelt behind the stage and cried. I felt I had failed God for my lack of faith. Suddenly, the pastor with the mike called for me and said, look at this lady she wants to testify. I heard her say in a loud voice in Spanish "Dios me tiro una piedra." In English I heard, "God threw a rock at me." The pastor insisted that I should let her testify. I was in panic mode. I started to see the headlines. "God throws rocks in the sports stadium." The pastor kept insisting that she should testify. I finally told the pastor "Por favor, Dios no tira piedras," which in English means, "Please, God does not throw rocks." He answered, "Ella está diciendo, Dios me estiro la pierna," (God has stretched (grown) my leg). My Spanish was so bad that I misunderstood. In Spanish it sounds almost the same. She was born with a withered leg, and when she heard the message, she looked at her leg and believed that God was healing her. She was born with a leg that did not develop correctly. Right before her eyes, her leg was restored and healed. That night, there was an explosion of miracles. All sorts of diseases went away, and people were healed of all kinds of sickness. The next day, the headlines read: "UNBELIVABLE MIRACLES HAPPENING IN THE STADIUM; BUT THEY ARE TRUE!"

From there, we went to another city to hold another crusade. A newscaster interviewed me. He was an unbeliever and accused me of deceiving people. He said that we gringos came and paid people to lie and make believe that they were healed. He then asked for permission to stand by my side and interview the people that were supposedly healed. I agreed. That night, the first person that Jesus healed was a blind lady that was his neighbor. He became a believer that same night. Every subsequent night, he stood by my side while I prayed for the sick. He looked like my assistant evangelist.

To be a faithful conduit, you must take care of yourself.

Your body is always at work. It produces new cells, pumps blood, takes in oxygen and much more. Moses was attracted to the burning bush because the fire did not consume the bush. The ministry should not cause burnout.

If you do not take care of your body and take precautions, you will cause harm to your body and mind. Many pastors suffer strokes and heart attacks starting in their 50's. You must obey the scriptures that say, "Be anxious for nothing."

You must learn how to enjoy the ministry and not to carry the load. Give it to God. The church will go on without you. Take extended vacations. Christ took the disciples to rest after their great revival meetings. Because of the many people coming and going, they did not even have a chance to eat. He said to them, *"Come with me by yourselves to a quiet place and get some rest."* Mark 6:31 (NIV)

Take at least one month a year. I believe that as the pastor, you deserve an executive allotment of a one-month vacation. Take at least one day a week for total relaxation. You are human. Your body is limited. Exercise is important if you want to maximize your years of service. The Bible does not say that it has no profit. It says it profits little (1 Timothy 4:8). A little is better than nothing.

Also build yourself. Attend conferences that minister to ministers. You are also a sheep and need to be fed. Read books that will edify your spirit and refresh your heart. Do all you can to help your body, mind and soul and then...Give it to God and go to sleep!

Eddie Rodriguez

What are your thoughts about this chapter? What stood out? What areas need to change?

Chapter 8
Have God's Heart

If God is your partner, make your plans big.
D.L. MOODY

"And I will give you shepherds according to my heart, who shall feed you with knowledge and understanding."
Jeremiah 3:15 (ASV)

As ministers of the gospel, we need to follow our leader, Jesus Christ. We need to do His will and not ours. This is especially important for those that have followers. As a leader, you will influence many to the correct or wrong path. Our constant prayer should be to have the heart of God. Look at His mandate and envelope your whole being in His heart. Let His compassion and love become your guiding force. When you have God's heart, you start to have big ideas and you become fearless. Others will judge you as being arrogant and presumptuous. Why, because..."God is a big God." He is waiting for His ministers to do great and mighty exploits in His name.

When David went to the camp to give his brothers their lunch, he heard Goliath challenge the Israelites. He immediately wanted to fight him. His brothers accused him of being arrogant and malicious. His brothers were judging David's heart (1 Samuel 17:28). Yet, God said that David's heart was according to His heart (1 Samuel 13:14 and Acts 13:22). That's the way others might see a minister with God's heart. Your heart should be according to God's heart. You start to believe God for great and mighty projects. You will have a heart like a fearless lion. People will look at you and say, "Who do you think you are?"

God's heart will give you supernatural love.

You will love the unlovable. When others offend you, you will cry out "Father, forgive them." You will weep for the lost and your church's spending will reflect your priorities.

You will have a great love for Children and Youth.

Your church will be a place that children and youth will love to be in. They will have life changing-memories. The Youth and Children's Ministry will be a priority. The church has to have Children and Youth Pastors. These should be one of the first ministers that receive financial help. If you cannot afford to give them a full-time salary, give them a stipend.

According to the Barna Group Study, this is the most important time to evangelize. "For years, church leaders have heard the claim that nearly nine out of ten Christians accept Jesus as their Savior before the age of 18. If that statistic was accurate in the past, it no longer depicts U.S. society. The current Barna Study indicates that nearly half of all Americans who accept Jesus Christ as their Savior do so before reaching the age of 13 (43%); and that two out of three born again Christians (64%) made that commitment to Christ before their 18th birthday. One out of eight born-again individuals (13%), made their profession of faith while they were 18 to 21 years old. Less than one out of every four born-again Christians (23%) embraced Christ after their twenty-first birthday. Barna noted that these figures are consistent with similar studies it has conducted during the past twenty years."[1]

It has been proven that childhood experiences determine what they feel emotionally as they mature. Sometimes they feel negative towards things, but don't know why. Many of our children and youth leave the church, never to return. All they remember is that they were considered a nuisance. They were told to sit still and behave.

You must have a kid-friendly church.

When the disciples rebuked the children, Jesus said, "Let them be" (Luke 18: 15-17). I am sure the disciples were not happy with the way the children were behaving, and yet Jesus was not bothered. He loves children more then you could imagine. I've always strived to have a church where children are loved, and where they are acknowledged. I always make sure not to only shake the hands of the parents, but also of the children. I believe we've accomplished having a kid-friendly church when I see and hear the children telling their parents that they do not want to leave when the service is finished.

Young people need a lot of attention.

They are in a stage in their lives where they are extremely social. Friends are of utmost importance to them. They are thinking of dating and even marriage. Flirting is part and parcel of their social life. They are trying to figure out their future careers, and their purpose in life. If the church fails to provide a busy social life for their youth, their unsaved friends will draw them in. Many times, it's difficult for the older generation to accept the ways of the new generation. We like different styles of music and fashion. I remember observing our youth worship team. I didn't like the way some of the boys would sing and shake their heads, so that their long hair would swoosh from side-to-side. I felt that they were showing off. I decided to approach them and correct them. On my way to speak to them, the Holy Spirit spoke to my heart, and I heard Him say, "Leave them be. They're young. It's part of their youth." The Youth Pastor has so much to do for his youth. You must understand the important role that the Youth Pastor has in the future of the church.

You must have a bold and fearless heart.

Exercise kingdom authority. All principalities and governments have been put under the feet of Jesus.

When I was a pastor at Love Tabernacle in West Palm Beach, FL, the Lord laid in my heart to put up a tent in the parking lot of the church building. The problem was that there were laws against putting up a tent for meetings within the city limits. Word got to the local pastors, and they called me and advised against it. One of the local pastors said that he tried for 7 years and the city would not allow it. In obedience to the Holy Spirit, I went to the City Engineer and asked for permission. She sent me to the Fire Chief, and he sent me to the Police Chief. The Police Chief sent me back to the City Engineer. The City Engineer looked baffled and finally gave me the go-ahead to put up the tent. God confused them all, so that we could obey His leading. While we were erecting the tent, the Fire Inspector came and demanded to speak with me. He asked me for permits. I told him I did not have anything written, but the city gave me the go-ahead to put up the tent. He began to inform me that it was illegal. I let him know that we had spent over $20,000 and if he ordered me to put it down, I would sue the city for that amount being that the City Engineer had given me permission to do so. He called the City Engineer and inquired about this. When he hung up, he just looked at me a little dumbfounded and told me to just continue with the tent. We had it up for 45 days and 400 people responded to the gospel. Many were healed and delivered. God is in control.

One year, an Evangelist named Yiye Avila came to Yonkers, New York. I had to go to the Parks and Recreation Commissioner to ask if we could use the local sports-park. It had bleachers and was perfect for the crusade. His response was that it would be impossible because that particular week was booked for little league games and Olympic tryouts. He was called out of his office, and in that moment I prayed, "God you're the owner of all things. In Jesus name, I claim that week for your kingdom's work." He walked back in, and with a puzzled look, grabbed an eraser and removed all the activities that were to take place that week. He turned around, scratched his head, and said "Pastor, you can have that week."

The building that we were considering to purchase, in West Palm Beach, was not zoned as a house of worship. When I started to negotiate the purchase of this building, I got calls from various pastors who advised me against the purchase of the building. One pastor had put a deposit to purchase the building, and fought the zoning board to rezone it for church use. He spent over $200,000 on lawyer fees, etc., to no avail. But, the Holy Spirit kept nudging me. When I finally signed the contract, I was deeply concerned. I did something that I would advise against. I'm a Real Estate broker and I would've never done this on my own. The seller said that this was now my problem, and if I couldn't get it rezoned, I would be stuck with the property. We paid $1.8 million, (money that we didn't have).

Under the new covenant, we are all filled with the Holy Spirit therefore we are not led by a prophet because the whole church is spirit-filled. When I presented the possibility of purchasing this building to the congregation, I painted a very negative picture. I knew that the Lord was leading me, but I wanted to make sure that they understood what we were up against. As I said in previous chapters, we are to submit one to another, therefore, this to me, would be a final confirmation. I presented the congregation an impossible scenario. We had in our present building a monthly, mortgage payment of $8,000 that we could hardly pay. We would now have another $20,000 monthly payment. We needed approximately $250,000 for renovations on this new purchase, and we had zero balance in our savings. They voted to go ahead and purchase it. My brother in-law asked me after the meeting, "Why did you speak as if you were against it?" I replied, "As the pastor of this church, I didn't want to influence them. I wanted to make sure that this move was in accordance to the prompting of the Holy Spirit. I learned years ago that when something is God's will, a praying church will know it."

The day I finalized the deal and received the ownership of the property, I walked in through the front door and started to doubt. As I looked around that 19,000 square foot building, I saw an impossible task. It was destroyed. It had been without use for over seven years. The walls and windows were all broken. The electricity was a mess. I had gone to architects and engineers, and they all were charging "an arm and a leg" to try to rezone and submit architectural plans. I started to weep and asked my Lord if I had truly been led by Him, or was I delusional. At that moment, a gentleman walked in and asked me if he could look around. After observing the place, he approached me and said "Pastor, I can get you the zoning within 30 days." I looked at him and thought "You must think I am a fool." I asked him, with a slight attitude, "How much is the charge? He responded, "Not a penny. I owe God much more than this." I don't know if I believed him at that moment, but it brought tears to my eyes. He later said that when he walked out of that building, he was shaking and asked himself, "Why did I say that?" He was not only able to change the zoning, but also got us the certificate of occupancy. How did he do it? I don't have a clue. He also did it in 21 days instead of 30. Donations and volunteer workers started to come in from unexpected sources. I was emotionally moved to see how God made this happen.

There is a verse in scripture that states the following advice that Jesus gave to his disciples "Don't feed your pearls to the swine" (Matthew 7:6-8). Meaning that if someone doesn't want to receive your message, then don't bother giving it to him or her. I see a spiritual principle in this teaching. God will not reveal his treasures to people that He knows will not believe Him. As God's minister, you must have an obedient heart. Only then will you be able to do His exploits in His name. If your heart and mind is open to receive His awesome plans, then and only then will He start leading you into the great things He wants you to do.

The kingdom of God must be taken by force.

Walk in total obedience. Do not depend on your meager resources but depend on His unlimited resources. There is nothing impossible for those who believe. You need to understand that with God's heart, you don't think out of the box, you think without a box. You don't let your past, your culture or your paradigm get in the way of the prompting of the Holy Spirit.

I have a personal opinion of what will happen when we stand before our King. He will have two books to show you. One will be of your life, and the other of what it could've been if you had believed Him for greater things. I imagine that the latter one will be much thicker than the former. My goal and prayer is that both would be equal in size. If God has called you to be a minister in His kingdom, walk boldly, humbly and in the Spirit. Always obey the leading of the Holy Spirit. If you do, you will see the glory of God, and He will open doors no man can shut. Pray that your heart will be according to God's heart.

What are your thoughts about this chapter? What stood out? What areas need to change?

Chapter 9
Give God Glory

*I give all the glory to God.
It's kind of a win-win situation.
The glory goes up to Him
and the blessing falls down on me.*
GABBY DOUGLAS
(Olympic Gold Medal Winner)

If there is a sin that God quickly reacts to is pride. It happens when you rob Him of His glory.

He quickly punished Nebuchadnezzar (Daniel 4:30-33), for this sin by making him eat grass like a beast. An angel killed Herod (Acts 12:23), when he tried to get the glory. We must be careful and always depend on Him.

Don't have a haughty spirit.

Pride comes before the fall (Proverbs 16:18). Jesus associated Himself with the poor and marginalized. He walked among the people. I can't see Christ hiding in an office so he would not be bothered by people. He gave His full attention to those that approached Him. His love was manifested in His walk and talk. He constantly gave the Father all the glory.

It's important to let others see that it is God's doing!

In one of my crusades, there was an explosion of miracles. Great faith had taken the hearts of all that were there that day. As I was ministering in the prayer line, the people would tell me their ailment. I would tell them that they were already healed and to examine themselves. They would search for the ailment, whether it was a tumor, a withered extremity, a deaf ear, etc. They would discover that they were healed. Truly, Jesus was present. I didn't even have to pray for them. During that time, the Lord stopped me. I Saw Jesus before the tomb of Lazarus. I heard Him say as He lifted His eyes to heaven,

> *"Father, I thank you that you have heard me. I knew that you always hear me, but I said this for benefit of the people standing here, that they may believe that you sent me."*
> John 11:41-42 (NIV)

I immediately understood that God wanted me to let the people see me pray so that they would know that it was He and not I healing them. He will not share His glory with anyone. We must go out of our way to make sure that people know that it's Him and not us that deserves all the glory and honor.

Make Sure Your Motives are Pure.

These are some of the characteristics of pride and self-glory:

1. When you preach without a prayer life. You feel you are sufficient enough to speak without seeking God's word for the church.

2. You want a bigger building and a larger crowd to compete with some other preacher or church.

3. You think that your church is the only church that God has given the city.

Watch your heart.

Confess your pride before the Lord. Always consult with God in prayer over your decisions. Listen to those around you, and always consider the advice of others (Proverbs 11:14). Have someone in your life that can hold you accountable. Walk humbly before the Lord. And always let the light shine on Him and not you.

Walk humbly before the Lord does not mean to belittle yourself or your ministry.

You must honor your ministry and recognize that you are an ambassador of the Kingdom of God. You are a man or woman of great authority. But you are also, all of the above, because of Him. It's because of who He is. It's ours by his unfailing grace and mercy.

> *"The twenty –four elders shall fall down before Him who sits on the throne, and shall worship Him that lives for ever and ever, and shall cast their crowns before the throne, saying, "You are worthy, our Lord and our God, to receive glory and honor and power: for you created all things, and by your will existed and were created."*
>
> Revelation 4:10-11 (ASV)

You achieve success in your life by God's grace. You should do absolutely nothing without God's prompting and grace. You are blessed to be a vessel that honors God and walks in obedience. As a norm, you should always wait on Him for direction and deployment. As a spiritual leader, the biggest responsibility you have is to those that follow your lead.

Be faithful in your calling and to your Lord.

Eddie Rodriguez

What are your thoughts about this chapter? What stood out? What areas need to change?

Chapter 10
Bless and Protect

*When you focus on being a blessing,
God makes sure that you are always blessed in abundance.*
JOEL OSTEEN

You bless and protect your congregants by:

1. Praying for them constantly.
2. Teaching them God's heart (His Word)
3. By actions

Let's explore these protection points.

Pray for Them

Paul states that he always presented his sheep in prayer (Ephesians 1). He prayed very specific prayers. We see them throughout his writings.

Jesus constantly prayed for His disciples. We see this especially in the book of John 17: 6-26. Jesus knew that Peter was going to be attacked by Satan. He prayed to the Father that his faith would not faint and that his trial would make him stronger (Luke 22:32). Samuel told the people of Israel that he would sin if he didn't pray for them (1 Samuel 12:23).

When you intercede for your congregation, God will lead you to pray for specific situations that the members of your church might be going through. When this happens, I've found it to be a helpful and an uplifting experience, for that specific person, especially if you call them and tell them how the Holy Spirit moved you to pray for them. Also remember to intercede for all those who are in your community, those who will be reached by your church.

One afternoon I was in prayer in my room. All of a sudden, I saw the face of one of my neighbors in tears. I immediately felt an urge to go to her house. I asked my wife to go knock on her door. My wife knocked on her door, but she didn't want to let her in. My wife saw she was crying and asked her if something was wrong. She went on to tell her how God had urged me in prayer to go to her house. She finally let my wife in. She had a bottle of wine and pills on her table and was about to commit suicide. We were able to lead her to Christ. She was in awe that God would love her so much that he led us to her at that precise moment.

Protect Them

You protect them by teaching them God's Word. Don't ever use the pulpit to scold or address a gossip. If you do, you feed the goats and starve the sheep. Feed the sheep. Goats will eat anything, but the sheep can die if they eat the wrong diet. Do not occupy the pulpit if you're angry. Check your heart and make sure you speak with love and tenderness. In my 50 years in ministry, I've seen when there's a negative situation among the sheep, the new converts are oblivious of it. By speaking of the negative situation from the pulpit, you only make it worse. Just focus on feeding the sheep. Their Father "God" has put them under your ministry. He expects you to feed them and protect them. If you fail to do this, He will do what any good parent will do. If you put your children in a daycare and you discover that they are not properly cared for, you will put them somewhere else. Teach them God's word, and by doing so, they will grow healthy. I believe that this is one of the most important things you can do for their protection. Many false doctrines have come, and many more will rise up in the last days. The only anchor that will protect them is their knowledge of God's word.

I spoke to an officer that specialized in identifying counterfeit money. I asked, "How many counterfeits have you seen?" He answered, "None." He went on to tell me that the counterfeits are always changing. They focus on knowing the real money, this way they could identify when the false one shows up, because they've studied the real one.

Action

You must actively be involved in their lives to protect them. My dad, who is 92 years old, was a pastor for many years. One day, as I was driving him around, he looked very pensive. Out of the blue, he said, as if talking to himself, "I wasn't a good preacher but, I was a good pastor." If he saw that a member was not at church on Sunday, the next day he would go visit their homes or the hospital. He constantly watched to see who was weakening in their faith. Every morning, at 5am, I would see my dad on his knees praying for the church members. This is truly the highest calling. We know one pastor cannot do it all. In order to be good shepherds, we must increase our pastoral staff to help and protect the sheep as the church grows.

While walking on one of the main streets in Yonkers one day, I saw a member of my church. She hadn't been to our service in a while, and I had encouraged her to go to church more often. All of the sudden, she saw her husband with his mistress. She turned around and ran towards them. The mistress took out a knife, and they were going to have a physical altercation. There I was, a little concerned, as I knew that this was not going to end well. I did not want to get in the middle of a catfight. I felt I had to do something. I walked up to the wife and held her hand gently. I asked her to come with me. As I walked her away from the situation, she pleaded with me to let her go. She wanted to fight with this other girl. I thought to myself, "She's bluffing. I'm not pulling her or holding her tightly." If she wanted to, she could have easily let go of my hand and go fight. Later that week, she went to church and testified that when I touched her, her body went limp and she felt totally drained. She recognized that God had intervened on her behalf. A visit, a phone call or a touch from a pastor makes a world of difference in the life of a person.

Scripture clearly teaches that we do not lord over them.

You should provide an example of what a Christian should be so that they can imitate your conduct (1 Peter 5: 2-3). As we walk in the high calling we must always have in mind that we will give account to our Heavenly Father concerning those that he put under our care. (Hebrews 13: 7 & 17)

Your conduct, above everything else, is what will teach them how to live.

It will help them prioritize what is important. As an example to follow, you must let your light shine. Do you want to have a church that worships? They must see you give worship the importance you want from them. I've seen many pastors stay in their office during worship, only to come out when it is time to preach. Some churches allow meetings during their worship time. Some even say that the preaching is the most important moment in the service, but worship is just as important. We must give as much respect and importance to the time of worship as we do to the preaching of the word. A church that worships in spirit and in truth brings down the glory of the Lord.

"But thou art holy, O thou that inhabitest the praises of Israel." Psalm 22:3. (KJV)

The pastor should worship along with the congregation. Only this will teach them the importance you give to worship. No one should be allowed to hold any meetings during worship. Through your conduct, you will show the congregation the importance there is in worship.

Do this in joy.

You cannot save or change anyone. Just love them. Be an example and know that God is the only one that can save and transform. Remember, not even Jesus was able to please all of his disciples. Judas betrayed him and backslid. We are no better than our Lord and Savior. Focus on the sheep.

There are many distractions in ministry, therefore, you must be diligent and focused on what is important. Prioritize, and stay focused on what is important.

What could be more important than winning the lost, and keeping the sheep grounded in His will?

Eddie Rodriguez

What are your thoughts about this chapter? What stood out? What areas need to change?

Chapter 11
Focus

*Any church that is not seriously
involved in helping fulfill
the Great Commission,
has forfeited its biblical right to exist.*
OSWALD J. SMITH

When I was in Sales, I noticed that the ones that looked and acted the angriest were the ones that bought. I had to put aside my defense mechanisms, and focus on the goal: sell, sell, and sell.

As a minister, you must focus on the bigger picture.

My job is to point them to Christ. Everything else is secondary. The parable of the Good Samaritan shows it clearly (Luke 10:25-3). The wounded man was passed by. Two religious leaders walked by and didn't stop to help. The Levite and the priest were probably on their way to a religious event. They were on church business. They had lost their focus. I'm sure that what they had to do was important. Whereas, the layperson from another denomination stopped, even though, he also had other things to do. That route was transited by people with business elsewhere. The Samaritan stopped because he saw a fellow human being in need. He gave priority to someone else's pain. That took precedence above all other pressing needs.

Remember, it's about souls.

You can get so caught up in religious responsibilities, that you become a professional clergy who does good religious things and forgets what moved you to ministry.

Which brings me to ask you…what makes you think you're called?

The most compelling sign that you are urged to be a minister is your deep concern and love for the souls of men. You see how lost mankind is, and you are compelled to tell them of this glorious gospel.

If you want to be a minister because you like to talk, or because you like the prestige, your motives are misdirected. Consider another field of work. What drives and fuels us to become ministers is our compassion and love for people (1 Corinthians 9:26). Your desire is to do what's in the heart of God, to point the lost to the cross at any cost.

Let's go back to the parable of the Good Samaritan. When he took him to the inn, he gave the innkeeper enough money to take care of the wounded man. Then he said, "If you spend more than this, when I return I will repay you." (Luke 10:35)

Go beyond of what is expected of you.

Be ready to sacrifice for the souls. When Christ returns he will reward you. In my first pastorate I had a member that tried my patience. He always criticized and complained. He was part of the worship team as a percussionist. He played an instrument known as a güiro. (It's a dried calabash that is indented with horizontal ridges. You play it with a ramrod that has metal prongs sticking out of it. You brush it to the rhythm.) That was about the time when the churches started to include electrical guitars. Well, he felt left out, so he put a microphone in the "güiro." You could imagine the disastrous noise it emitted. I was at my wits end. I was about to speak to him when the missionary of the church took me aside and said, "Pastor before you speak to him, allow me to give you the background of how he got here. He used to be known as the crazy man of Yonkers. He would spend all his time going up and down the streets yelling and talking to himself. One day he wandered into church. He came forward for prayer and was demon possessed. We spent three days fasting in the church with him until he was finally delivered. Please pastor, be kind towards him." That really opened my eyes to see the value of a soul, and helped me to be tender towards him.

After being in the pastorate for some years, I was pretty

comfortable with my pastoral duties. I was also serving in my denomination as an executive officer. One Sunday after the service, a young couple approached me. The young man and his wife were in their early twenties. She had beautiful red, curly hair, and he looked burdened. He went on to share with me their situation. They got married in Puerto Rico and had two children. She was an innocent, naive country girl. They moved to Florida and her cousin insisted that she should try a drug named "Crack." This drug is a highly, potent-derivative of cocaine. She immediately became obsessed with it. She went to the streets and got into prostitution, so that she could buy more drugs. He pleaded with me to take her off the streets. I asked her if she wanted to leave that life, and she also pleaded that she needed help. We said the prayer of salvation. Afterwards, I looked at my calendar and noted that I had other commitments for Monday and Tuesday, but advised that I could take her to a Christian rehab on Wednesday. I told them to meet me at church on Wednesday at 10 am. Wednesday came and they didn't show up. That night as I watched the evening new, her face popped up on the screen. They found her body in a ditch, riddled with bullets. I was so overwhelmed with sadness. I realized, at that moment, that my priorities were off-kilter. It shook me to the core. It's about souls. All else is secondary.

Missions

If we make His priority ours, we will begin to walk in another dimension. Make His mandate, your mandate. Go into the world and make disciples. Your church programs and giving should reflect that mandate. If it truly does, your missions giving should be ridiculously enormous. Your members will be soul winners. Nothing will hinder your vision. He will give you all that you need to do His kingdom work.

Spreading the gospel is not only preaching. It is also doing. For many years, some in the church have criticized compassion ministries. Some have even said that the church shouldn't get involved in anything else but preaching. They have ministered under the false pretense that social outreach was a contradiction to the mission. That is a totally wrong doctrine. Even Jesus fed the multitude out of compassion, and tended to his mother's social need while on the cross. We must, as ministers, minister to the whole man. We must feed the hungry; have rehab centers; rescue people from sex slavery; start hospitals; open schools in places of need; and the list goes on.

Don't forget what Jesus taught,

> *35 For I was hungry and you gave me something to eat, I was thirsty and you gave me something to drink, I was a stranger and you invited me in, 36 I needed clothes and you clothed me, I was*

> *sick and you looked after me, I was in prison and you came to visit me.*
> Matthew 25:35-36 (NIV)

This screams at the church "Where were you when I needed food, clothes or a visit?" Love should not be just an emotion or words. It should be an action. What does it matter if you hug a hungry child and not feed him or a naked person and not cover him? By extending a helping hand, you preach the most powerful sermon. It will open their hearts to hear what you have to say. Then, they will hear the message of the cross because they saw it in action first.

This is what true ministry is all about. It is not only to do, but also to teach others to do the same. This is what determines the future of the church.

It's not only about what you do, it's about inspiring others to feel the same compassion and responsibility.

Eddie Rodriguez

What are your thoughts about this chapter? What stood out? What areas need to change?

Section 4
Ministry

Chapter 12
Leadership Models

Leadership Models
*Leaders become great, not because of their power,
but because of their ability to empower others.*
John Maxwell

Let's look at the three styles of leadership. All of these styles have their use in the church. These three different levels progressively lead to the final goal of every church… to produce leaders.

All three have their season.

Three Leadership Models

The first type of Leader is positioned in the front of the sheep and everyone is following him. He does it all. He is the whole orchestra.

This style is necessary in the beginning of church planting.

When you start a church, you have very little choice but to follow the first model. Everyone is new, and you might not have a support team. In a church startup, you might have to do it all. This may include cleaning the meeting hall, to turning off the lights when church is finished. This should be a very short season.

The second type of Leader is among the sheep...the people. He is friends with each of them, and is involved in their daily walk.

This second level is when the pastor starts a more intensive training. The members start to discover their purpose and function in the body of Christ.

This is the time to build your flock. The group you have is still small enough where you could be more involved in their growth. You should be training leaders and disciple makers. This model will overwhelm you. As the church grows, the members will expect you to be with each of them. If you stay there too long, you will create an unhealthy dependence on you.

The third type of Leader is behind the sheep. He urges and motivates them. His eyes are on all.

This is the final goal of a leader. Everyone knows their function, and your role becomes more of a coach to motivate and encourage.

This is when the church has a clear vision, and you have equipped them to fulfill their part in the body of Christ. You are there to motivate, coach and advise. This is a mature church that has come to the realization that they are also responsible for each other. It is no longer the job of the pastor alone. They too, have a mission to fulfill, and they have already defined their function in the body of Christ. If you stay too long on the first model, it will cause burnout and stress.

The congregation doesn't want you to smell like sheep.

They want you to give off a heavenly aroma; a fragrance of someone that has been in God's presence. If you smell like sheep, they will bite you. My older brother was a candidate for his Doctorate PHD when he told me "Eddie when I go to church I don't want to hear just another dissertation. I hear that from the professors. I come to church to receive a word from God.

Let's look at the passage, my sheep hear my voice. John 10: 1-3

Many times I've heard preachers say, that when our voice is heard, the sheep will follow. But, nothing can be further from the truth. In this parable, Jesus is the voice. It's the Holy Spirit that will ring true in the hearts of the sheep. Where are we, the pastors, in this parable? We are the "gatekeepers." We open or shut the door.

Let's talk about the role of the pastor as the gatekeeper.

Our responsibility as the gatekeepers is to make sure that the Holy Spirit is given preeminence in our midst. We need to keep watch so that those that occupy our pulpits will bring a word from the Lord. We must make sure that we don't shut out what the Holy Spirit wants to do, but also close that door tight to demonic and carnal influences.

As a young pastor, one of my greatest regrets was that I allowed some preachers to occupy the pulpit, and that caused harm to my congregation. Since then, I have been more diligent and cautious. I do not get in the way nor allow anyone else to get in the way of what the Holy Spirit wants to do. Be very careful as to whom you allow to preach and teach to your church. Do not feel obligated to invite someone just because they asked you to invite them.

Let's recap the three levels of leadership.

These three levels are phases seen in the overall development of the church. The first level is for the new converts. In the second level, you help them discover their purpose in the body of Christ. Once they have discovered that purpose, you go into the third phase. You become a facilitator so that they can fulfill their purpose. They will also disciple others.

Eddie Rodriguez

What are your thoughts about this chapter? What stood out? What areas need to change?

Chapter 13
Equip the Front Line

*The Christian life is not a playground.
It's a battleground.*
AUTHOR UNKNOWN

Scripture talks about a battle. We are at war, (Matthew 11:12) and this war is real. Don't be mistaken. Many are wounded and even killed. It is a constant battle against the principalities of darkness (Ephesians 6:12). Satan strategizes on how to defeat the soldiers of God's kingdom.

I heard many teachings as a young preacher. It went like this. "Ministers are in the front lines of the battle." I believed this for many years. How wrong was I!!!

As ministers, we are surrounded by believers. They address us as Pastor or Reverend. When we are present, they watch what they say and how they say it. We spend the day doing God's work, whether it is visiting the sick, praying or studying the bible.

On the other hand, the members of our congregations are among non-believers, and some haters of the gospel. They are constantly being exposed to temptations and ridicule, circumstance that we as ministers are not exposed to. They come on Sundays, wounded, beaten and exhausted by the struggle.

First of all, our church members are in the Front Line!

What do they need? They need to be healed, refueled, motivated and comforted. They are in the front lines. We should be the hospital motivating and healing the soldiers of the Lord. We need to supply them with the necessary weapons and nourishment.

Let's not forget. Any decent enemy will try to cut the supply source and destroy the infrastructure.

The enemy knows that he can demoralize the troops by doing this. We must be cognizant of our role. When they come to you on Sunday, they need to hear a word from heaven. They need to be healed and motivated. How many times do they get beat up by the enemy during the week only to go to church and get beat up by the preacher?

I look back at the battles of Israel. While God's soldiers fought, Moses was on the mountain with his arms lifted in intercession. While his hands were lifted, God's army won, but when he lowered his hands they would start losing (Exodus 17:11). You must intercede for those that God has put before you. They come on Sundays believing that while they were in the valley, you were in the mountain getting a word from the Lord for them. They will know if you were in the mountain. They will know when you speak the word of the Lord to their hearts.

The congregation doesn't want you to smell like sheep, and God wants you to protect them.

They want their pastor to be in God's presence while they are in the valley of the battle. When they sit in the pew, they want to hear a word from heaven, coming from someone that's been in the mountain. Be careful not to ignore your time with God. Your first priority is your relationship with the Lord, not with the people. In order to have the mind of God, you must get away from the noise around you. The negativity around you can cancel God's mind in your heart.

Paul sent them with letters of reference.

Make sure that the invited preachers will edify the Front Line. The Bible clearly outlined the method used by the Apostles. One of the most misinterpreted gifts of the Holy Spirit is the gift of discernment. The reference to this gift is used by many to manipulate the pastor into inviting himself or herself to their pulpit. Many preachers will say "Don't you have the gift of discernment?" They imply that if you need references, then you're not spiritual. The early church was very clear. They sent their emissaries with letters.

Examples: The letter sent to Philemon about Onesimis (see Romans 16:1-2). Also, throughout his writings, Paul recommended different ministers to the local congregation.

These are some of the things you should tell a preacher that you do not know.

1. I need to have a relationship with you.

2. I need two letters of reference. One from your present pastor and the other from the pastor that helped you in your first walk in Christ, (if different).

3. I'm not interested in a letter from a pastor telling me how God used you in his church. That doesn't speak of your fruits, only of your gifts. Your gifts do not say anything of your personal life or doctrine. Jesus said you would know them by their fruits.

In this war, our General is God the Father, Son and Holy Spirit. He provides the logistics and plans of attack and defense. The ministers are what this word "ministers" implies. You are to serve.

We are the doctors, nurses, the healers and encouragers. Our church members are the ones on the Front Lines.

Eddie Rodriguez

What are your thoughts about this chapter? What stood out? What areas need to change?

Chapter 14
Empower Others

We raise children with the hope that they will mature into independent individuals who will leave their own legacy.
EDDIE RODRIGUEZ

Scripture tells us that the minister's purpose is to equip the saints to enter into the fullness of Christ.

My goal as a minister is to see that every member in the church fulfills their calling.

The pastor is a facilitator. We must help the saints understand and do what God has called them to do, so they may discover their gifts and talents and function in God's Kingdom.

> *"And he gave some to be apostles; and some, prophets; and some, evangelists; and some, pastors and teachers; for the perfecting of the saints, unto the work of ministering, unto the building up of the body of Christ:"*
> Ephesians 4:11-12 (ASV)

This is referring to the body of Christ, which is the church. Your congregation is part of that church. Sometimes you equip so that they can GO. Do not retain the called to GO. You must not be selfish. Sometimes you will train so that your disciples can bless another congregation. You must have a kingdom mentality. What is a kingdom mentality? It's when you see that your job is not just to build your congregation, but to build other congregations, bless other congregations, and send missionaries to the four corners of the earth. You rejoice when other congregations grow.

Many churches are more like a cruise ship.

A small percentage, work; and the vast majority lounge and drink piña coladas. But, the church should be more like a battleship, where every single person has a job to do. No one lounges around. Everyone is essential in his or her job. It should be a carrier ship that sends warplanes with a specific mission, only to return to refuel, to go out again and again.

Many ministers take the load all on themselves. You should allow each member to have a vision for his or her lives.

> *"For as the body is one, and hath many members, and all the members of the body, being many, are one body; so also is Christ. For the body is not one member, but many. But now hath God set the members each one of them in the body, even as it pleased him. And if they were all one member, where were the body? But now they are many members, but one body.*
>
> 1 Corinthians 12:12, 14, 18-20 (ASV)

Our God is a creative God. He likes new things.

He said, "I will do a new thing." He wants to pour new wine into new wine skins. He said, "I want a new song." Jesus said "I will drink new wine." He was buried in a new tomb.

I have been surprised with what members of my church have accomplished. A church that has every member working in their purpose, can only grow healthy.

The danger and/or death of your joy and your ministry is when you micro-manage. You must delegate and trust those you have delegated to. Will they make mistakes? Of course, we all do. You will need to be there to coach and motivate them.

Never allow any leader to speak disparagingly of another leader.

One of the most important characteristics that I demand of everyone is that when they serve in the church, they are always to act and react in love. I do not allow a servant-leader to disrespect anyone. We are called to love.

As a young Christian, many times I heard pastors say, "If you don't agree with my vision, there's the door."

Well, one Sunday morning, I said those words to the church. When I got home, I went to pray. Immediately, the

Holy Spirit rebuked me. In my heart, and with clarity, I understood that this offended God. I prayed for forgiveness. In the next service, I stood before my congregation and humbly apologized for what I had said. There was an outpouring of love. The saints were deeply touched, and there was weeping and worship. A hug-fest broke out. You see pastor it's about love and compassion. It's every member functioning to fulfill God's purpose on this earth. The calling of God for every minister is to be a blessing to those around them. You are the conduit where God's word and love can flow to others.

Keep this in mind, they are God's children.

The same way a parent loves their children, so God loves His children. Again, if you take your children to a daycare and you find out that they are being mistreated and not well-fed, you will find another more loving and attentive daycare. Our Heavenly Father will do the same with His children. He will remove them and take them where they will be loved. So walk in love, and make sure you are feeding them healthy food. Always make sure that your heart is according to God's heart.

You have been given the responsibility to watch over His children. You are to feed them, comfort and encourage them by giving them a fresh word, especially when they are hurt or discouraged.

The scripture clearly says that you are to give account for their souls (Hebrews 13:11).

What are your thoughts about this chapter? What stood out? What areas need to change?

Chapter 15
Love People

*It's all summed up in one word "love."
It is the Holy Spirit's job to convict,
God's job to judge, and my job to love.*
BILLY GRAHAM

Spiritual Inspiration

Know that God loves you more than you can fathom. He is your protector, defender and your greatest advocate. He loves your family and will cover them under His wings. He will never give you more than you can carry. He allows mistakes, and remembers that we are just dust. He believes in you. He called you, knowing that you will make mistakes and fail. Those things will not take Him by surprise. Many times you will want to quit. That's normal. Trust in His grace. Goodness and mercy will follow you all the days of your life. He wants you to be joyful. He wants you to stay healthy, so that you can give many years of service. He will turn every curse spoken against you into a blessing. Learn how to rejoice when people talk about you.

Let me share some of my experiences of His love!

When my wife was pregnant with our third child, a woman knocked at our door at about 2 am. It was a member of the church we pastored. She was angry with me because her 22 year-old son wanted to get married, and I gave him my blessing. She was against him getting married. When I opened the door, she began to spew hateful words at my wife. She started cursing her pregnancy and cursed the unborn child. She began to say that the child would be born sick, and that it would be a sickly child all of her life. My wife was visibly shaken after those vitriolic words were vomited towards her. That curse was turned around, and the complete opposite occurred. Michelle was born so healthy, that the doctor came into the waiting room in shock. He began to inform me that Michelle looked like she was lifting weights. Her physique was exceptional. As a child, she was the healthiest of my three children. She never got sick, and that was the pattern in my whole life. Whenever someone spoke words to harm my family or me, God always turned it into a blessing. So rejoice and live surrounded by God's love.

Remember, this is God's church.

Don't walk around burdened. Only God can save marriages and people. All you need to do is pray for them, and love them the same way God loves you. God will watch over your family. We have learned that when the enemy throws an arrow at us, by the time it reaches us God turns it into a rose!

Years ago, before computers and cell phones, I went to South America for four weeks. I had four major crusades. I had a big concern, with my second child, Darlene. She was only three years old, and she wouldn't sleep until I gave her many kisses. She would ask me to kiss her and would say, again repeatedly before falling asleep. This really worried me and made me feel guilty over leaving my family for so long. I finally got a response from my wife. I had written her a letter where I asked her about Darlene. My wife informed me that the first night Darlene cried for a little while, but every night afterwards she would not cry. My wife asked her why she didn't cry anymore. Darlene answered, "Daddy comes into my room every night and gives me a lot of kisses." I lifted my tear-filled eyes and praised my loving Father. The fact that He would do this for my daughter was such a revelation of how deep God's love is for His servants and their family.

You must love people as much as God loves you.

If you cease to love people, the ministry will wear you down. God did not call you to change them nor to manipulate them.

There will always be people that will come against you.

You are not greater than Jesus. He had twelve disciples,

and one of the twelve went against Him. Yet, He still washed his feet, and did not kick him off the team.

The Apostle Paul knew that one of the dynamics of his happiness was people. He knew that if he caused them to lose their joy, he would also lose his. Therefore, he made sure that his words would always result in their joy being kept or restored (2 Corinthians 2:1-4).

Pastors, you must remember this dynamic in scripture. Make sure that you preach and teach with this in mind. A congregation that has a pastor that practices this dynamic is a strong congregation. The joy of the Lord is your strength (Nehemiah 8:10).

Don't forget that the tares and the wheat will grow together.

It's not your job to separate them. In His return, he will separate the tares from the wheat. He admonishes that by trying to root out the tares you might also root out the wheats. Matthew 13: 24-30

There was a man in the church that I pastored in Yonkers that was not acting right. I was going to confront him. I knew that this man's character was of the type that would leave the church when confronted. But, his actions were so egregious that I felt I had no choice. The night before I was to confront him, as I was in prayer, I had a very disconcerting vision. I saw this man leave the Lord, and his wife and children were crying as he forced them to follow him on his destructive path. The Lord opened my understanding. God's word to my heart was the following, "For the love of his family let him be." You must love as Jesus loves.

While I was the superintendent of my district, I counseled a minister that was out of control. He had been a major drug trafficker from Panama. He came from a violent past. When the Presbyter tried to correct some of his conduct towards his church, this pastor's reaction was blatantly disrespectful and threatening. I was asked to deal with this pastor. As he was talking to me, also with threatening words and anger, I was writing down all the reasons why he had to be removed from the pastorate. When he finished talking, I was about to read him that list. At that moment I heard in my spirit these words, "You forgot to write down one more item...that I love him." I tore the list and invited him to pray with me. We cried before the Lord and hugged each other.

Many souls will be sitting in your audience that will challenge your theology. For example, many will be in your pews that will have attractions to their same-sex. Homosexuality has become rampant in our society. The church will and is facing this challenge. Just have in mind the vision that God gave Peter at Simon the Tanner's house. He saw a sheet come down from heaven with unclean animals, and God told him to kill and eat. Peter was not comfortable with the idea, but God told him, "Do not call unclean what I have made holy."

We must understand that God loves the homosexual and lesbian community. I remember the night of the slaughter of the nightclub in Orlando, Florida. It was a gay club, and many were killed. I remember that day because that morning before it happened, the Holy Spirit quickened me with weeping to pray for the homosexual community. I know God loves them deeply, and we as a church must manifest God's love for them. The church has been guilty of speaking love but showing hate. We must let them know that God loves them. Their lifestyle does not exempt them from God's love. He died for them and declared them forgiven. Remember God is the only one that can change lives. Our job is to love.

As a 21st century church, we are facing humongous challenges, and we must understand that it is God's will for the church to love, pray for them, restore them and disciple them. Let God do the change and the transformation that only He can do. In the meantime, yes we must preach and teach God's plan for their lives, but we must do it in love. We must show them God's love through our actions. We must understand that God loves everyone and that His love is manifested through the church. We must fight in prayer and action for them.

When faced with a church split, don't let bitterness enter into your heart.

This is one of the strongest weapons that Satan will use against you. It is one of the most painful experiences you will experience. Love will overcome this weapon. As a pastor's son, I was exposed to many conversations that pastors had with each other. I remember hearing their stories of betrayal and church divisions. I noticed how some were still bitter and had lost their trust in having assistant pastors. I made up my mind, at that moment as a young aspiring-minister that I would never let bitterness or mistrust enter into my heart. I have experienced divisions and church splits. I have reacted in love. I have prayed for God to bless them. I have given them a seed offering to help them find a place. I have offered to donate chairs. I refused to fight or give in to bitterness. The important thing is that Christ is preached as expressed by the apostle Paul in Philippians 1:15-18.

I've had assistant pastors lead a group out to start another congregation without my blessing. I blessed them anyway. This did not stop me from having a pastoral team. I presently have nine individuals as part of my pastoral staff. You must not give in to anger and/or bitterness. This will only stunt your growth and take away your joy. It's in these trials that you will show the members true-life lessons.

Another life-changing example in my journey!

This young woman responded to an altar call. She accepted Christ as her personal Savior. She had a reputation of being a loose woman in our city. She became a handful in our church. We call that "half-baked" Christians. God had changed her, but she had a long way to go. She was still smoking and when she would come to church, she would always sit in the same spot. If anyone was seated in her spot of the bench, she would start yelling and demanding that they move. She would do this even in the middle of my sermon. The Deacons were fed up with her. The church back then was very legalistic, but God was dealing with me and showing me how legalism was not according to his heart. The Deacons asked me to do something about this situation. I told them to give her one more year to see if within that year she would change.

When the year was up, she was still doing the same things. I was on the pulpit with an invited Evangelist, Rev. Santiago Rios, who God used mightily with a prophetic ministry. I was anxious for the service to finish so that I could talk to this woman and give her an earnest correction. (It was going to be more like a verbal beating.) All of a sudden, Santiago Rios looked at me and pointed to that very woman and told me, "God is talking to me about that lady." I thought to myself, good. God is going to confirm what I'm going to do. Then he said "This is God's word for you. I have brought her to this church because you were going to be patient with her. If she would have gone to another church, she would have left a long time ago. I am still working in her life. Continue being patient."

This is what having love and the heart of God means.

What are your thoughts about this chapter? What stood out? What areas need to change?

Chapter 16
Speak Like Jesus

The length of a film should be directly related to the endurance of the human bladder.
ALFRED HITCHCOCK

Many pastors have stunted the growth of their congregation by having long services, and because of that, people will not come back to their church. By prolonging your service, you show lack of consideration. Many parents have small children that need attention. Some health issues have to be taken care of. Schedules have to be met. Sitting for such a long time can create health issues. The list can go on. The exception is if there is a great move of God birthed by the Holy Spirit. If this occurs, be mindful and dismiss with love those that need to go, and lovingly invite those that can stay, to do so. Your sermon should take all this in consideration. Paul said that we are not persuaded by many words but by the power of the gospel.

> "And my speech and my preaching were not in persuasive words of wisdom, but in demonstration of the Spirit and of power: that

> *your faith should not stand in the wisdom of men, but in the power of God."*
> 1 Corinthians 2:4-5 (ASV)

One of the biggest mistakes a preacher can make is to talk beyond what the Holy Spirit wants them to say.

Many preachers take a great message and destroy it by talking too much. We observe our Lord Jesus Christ in His delivery, and He was on point, short and powerful.

Even in the Old Testament God spoke succinctly and clearly. MENE TEKEL PARSIN" (Daniel 5:25), that was all and the prophet interpreted it almost verbatim.

One year I was invited to preach in this church, where the pastor was a famous lawyer. He had a congregation of thousands. It was in Puerto Rico. I had to preach in Spanish. Even though my parents were Puerto Rican, I was born and raised in New York. My Spanish was very limited. The little I knew was a mix of Spanish and English. It was "New Yorican" Spanish. I was in my early twenties and filled with insecurities. A member of his church picked me up at the airport and sat me in the back. The person did not speak to me. As we approached where I was staying, this person spoke up and said, "I don't know why the pastor invited you. We only get prominent speakers in our church." I was already feeling insufficient. You can imagine how those words made me feel. When I finally went to sleep, I had a horrifying dream. The pastor called me up to preach and did not allow me up on the stage. He told me to preach from the floor. I started to look for the Bible verse and couldn't find it. In the dream, the pastor was looking down at me from the pulpit, yelling hurry up!! I woke up in a cold sweat. I got on my knees and started to call upon God. I asked for strength and courage. God gave me a word that filled me with courage and strength. "I have given you a message. Don't try to impress man. Do not add nor take away from it. Just say what I want you to say, nothing more; nothing less." I share this with you so that you too can be filled with strength and courage.

The next day, I was seated in the tent (it was a tent crusade) and no one greeted me. The Pastor just walked past me and did not say a word. I was asked by one of the ushers if I was a pastor, and he proceeded to take me to the stage to sit with all the visiting pastors. As the time for the message got closer, the pastor started to introduce the speaker for the event. He spoke so well of him that I thought he had invited someone else and felt relieved. Then he presented me. I preached in my limited Spanish. I proclaimed the message God had put in my heart. I think I spoke no more than 25 minutes. When I made the call to repentance and to accept Christ, hundreds came to the stage weeping and crying. The pastor took the mike after I had finished ministering and said, "Many have asked me why I invited this kid to preach. Now you know why. I preach for an hour, and maybe two or three come up for salvation. This kid preaches just for a few minutes, and hundreds come to Christ". He invited me back year after year.

Preacher, God is not long-winded.

Learn how to deliver the message being succinct and with brevity. The people will be edified and will come back. Save the details, and the more in depth messages, for the midweek bible studies.

We must learn how to speak like Jesus spoke.

Eddie Rodriguez

What are your thoughts about this chapter? What stood out? What areas need to change?

Chapter 17
The Effective Message

*If Jesus preached the same message
ministers preach today,
He would never have been crucified.*
LEONARD RAVENHILL

**Christ had a message for the multitude...
Another for the 70...
One for the twelve...
Another for the three...
Another, just for one...**

This should be a pattern to follow.

When Jesus preached to the multitude, He spoke with brevity and illustrations called parables. But, He sometimes ministered all day and night. We must not forget; love for the people will compel you to make altar calls and take time to pray for people. Many times, we do the opposite of what Christ did.

**We preach all day, and do not minister.
The altar call is a rarity in some churches.**

Then, there were the more intimate lessons. I'm sure that

these were longer and more profound. I compare this to the midweek service. Here you disciple and mentor the faithful.

Then, He would speak to the twelve. These He walked with and shared His heart. The discipleship here was more personal. They were able to observe his every move and conduct.

You can't truly disciple every member of the church, but you can disciple some. I compare this to your pastoral team and your deacons. These are the ones that will be able to observe your conduct and life in a more intimate and personal way. So we see the model that Jesus gave us. It's a formula that will help us imitate and be fruitful.

One purpose behind this model was to, not only disciple, but to create disciple makers. Everyone understood that they too, must disciple others.

I believe that one of the biggest challenges is to keep the gospel message a central part of our proclamation.

You should always point to the cross and lift Jesus up in all your messages. This is where the transforming power lies.

> *"For the word of the cross is to them that perish foolishness; but unto us who are saved it is the power of God, but we preach Christ crucified, unto Jews a stumbling block, and unto Gentiles foolishness; but unto them that are called, both Jews and Greeks, Christ the power of God, and the wisdom of God.*

1 Corinthians 1:18, 23-24 (KJV)

When Christ said, "Do this in remembrance of me," the implication was clear. There will come a time when Christ will be a side-note in the church, and when in many pulpits we will hear all manner of speeches that sound more like a political or motivational session void of Christ, and the cross. The cross is the power and wisdom of God.

> *Jesus said, "If I be lifted up, I will draw all men unto me. And I, if I be lifted up from the earth, will draw all men unto myself. But this he said, signifying by what manner of death he should die."*
>
> John 12:32-33 (ASV)

The message of the cross should not be just for Easter and Holy week.

The message of the cross should be the center of the message. This was instilled in me as a five year-old child. One day, as I was walking into my room, I looked up and had an unusual vision. I remember it as if it was yesterday. I saw Christ on the cross. His face was in agony, as hands were raised towards him, mocking him. I was startled and afraid. I ran and grabbed my dad by his pants and was shaken. This vision has stayed with me my whole life. Many times when I speak of the cross I have this picture before me.

As an adult, I saw in a dream a beautiful flower with many

petals. I looked at it quickly, and then looked away. As I looked away, I heard a voice command me to look at the flower again. I gave it another quick glance. Again the tender voice told me to look. I understood that He wanted me to keep my eyes on the flower. As I stared, I realized that every petal had beautiful dimensions. Every petal had revelations that unfolded and, as I stared, I realized that the flower symbolized Jesus. Sometime later, I saw the same flower in a painting that was called a Chrysanthemum.

You must never give in to the message of what people want to hear. You must keep the message of the cross fresh and pertinent. It will draw all into the church. For the message to be fresh and pertinent, we must speak with anointing and revelation.

Be careful to communicate effectively and clearly.

Do not fall into the error of many orators. They use the platform to demonstrate how smart they are. They start to use very esoteric words. These are words that most people do not understand. Remember, you are speaking a life-changing, death and life message.

You don't yell about the chemical compounds of fire, when there is a danger of death. You yell, "Fire, fire!" so that people can run and save themselves. You are not to use the pulpit to project your abilities or education, but to exalt Jesus so that the listeners may fall in love with Christ.

As a 16 year-old evangelist, I was invited to a small town in Puerto Rico called Aguas Buena. We secured the plaza in the center of town. The first night I preached on the cross and God's love. Many came to the stage, contrite and repentant, to give their lives to Christ. A minister came up to me afterwards, and said that the church people did not like the message. The next day, I stood up and preached what I knew the church people liked. I started calling people sinners, adulterers, drunkards, etc. The church people were jumping and yelling praises. When I did the altar call, no one responded. The Holy Spirit whispered to my heart "Preach my love. I will convict the sin". Lesson learned.

> *"For now am I seeking the favor of men, or of God? Or am I striving to please men? If I were still pleasing men, I should not be a servant of Christ."*
>
>   Galatians 1:10 (ASV)

What are your thoughts about this chapter? What stood out? What areas need to change?

Section 5
Faith

Chapter 18
Trust & Finances

*God's work done God's way
will never lack God's provision.*
HUDSON TAYLOR

"El que invita...paga!"

One of the biggest challenges many ministers face, is finances. We have big dreams and ideas for projects. We look at our budget and our present income and, we either get discouraged and/or put our dreams on hold; or we start to demand the congregants to give or worse, we start to "sell snake oil."

You must have faith for finances.

You need to plan according to God's budget. In the year 2006, while pastoring A Place Called Hope Church, I was told that we were to receive a 17 million dollar donation. I started to dream about what I was going to do with that money. I thought of building a "City of Hope," a place that would minister and supply the spiritual and social needs of our community. All of the sudden, the donor's only child opposed the donation, and it never came. As I prayed, the Holy Spirit spoke to me, and I heard in a very clear thought. "You started to dream when you thought you were receiving that $17 million donation. I have given you much more. Don't stop dreaming". God used that experience to expand my vision.

Let me share a key that has never failed me.

Make sure it's a dream or goal that is in God's perfect will for you. It's a matter of obedience. Remember that verse.

> "So likewise ye, when ye shall have done all those things which are commanded you, say, We are unprofitable servants: we have done that which was our duty to do."
> Luke 17:10 (KJV)

If it's a project that God has led you to do, He will supply according to his riches, not yours. The quote that is used in the beginning of this chapter implies that the person that invited you to eat pays the bill. God owns all the riches of this world and beyond (Philippians 4:19). He will never ask you to do something, and then abandon you.

How do you know when it is God's will?

I've seen many ministers act, in what they called faith, and fail. Many have been taught to do whatever comes to mind, and if there's enough faith, you can demand from God, confess it and it will happen. NOT!! Faith is obedience. Faith is to have the courage to follow the leading of the Holy Spirit. Faith waits on God, no matter what happens (Luke 17:10). The father of faith, Abraham, left his land in obedience, not knowing where he was going.

As a young pastor in Yonkers, New York, we needed to move our church from the present building. As I was driving by a supermarket, I felt in my spirit that God wanted me to purchase that building. It had a bowling alley in the basement, and three small stores on the side. I got excited and told my board. Well lo and behold, someone else had bought it. I was so discouraged, and started to doubt what I had thought God had told me. All of the sudden, I got a call from the person that bought it. He sold it to us at half the price he paid. The building had some equipment that he needed, and now he had no use for it. Truly, God is awesome.

On Mother's Day 1976, after being in that building for approximately three years, my wife and I were driving towards the church, and saw all the people outside the building. In front of the door were two policemen standing guard, and not letting anyone in. The city declared the building to be not fit for a church. I inquired as to why now. The officers had no idea. They were just following orders. We were confronted with a persecution that lasted over a year. The city tried to expel Filipos Church from the map of Yonkers. I was threatened with jail time, and was blocked from having any type of church service. That included anywhere else that wasn't a church building. They would not issue a permit for a tent or any other venue. We had to have clandestine services. Many times, we would just meet in the alley of the church and start services until the police would show up and shut us down. Some churches in the area opened their doors, only to ask us to leave within weeks of being there.

We fought it in the local court, and the court decided in our favor. The city appealed to the Supreme Court and won. The judge wrought an opinion that was published in the local newspaper. He said that he was obligated to strike in favor of the city because of the way the law was written. These were laws that were put there to hinder bars and strip joints from having a free hand. Then he went on to say, that he felt that Filipos Church was being unjustly treated, and urged someone to investigate. Based on conversations overheard by members of the church that worked in City Hall, we got an idea as to why this persecution started. Weeks before that Mother's Day, we had a large crusade with Yiyé Avila, a Puerto Rican evangelist that God was using mightily. It was a citywide crusade, but all the permits were in the name of Filipos Church. I invited the Mayor and all the city officials. They were very religious, Roman Catholics. The evangelist asked the people to bring all their religious statues to the platform. The next day, the stage was filled with statues of Mary and every saint imaginable. Yiyé had, what he called, the holy hammer, and proceeded to smash all the statues. Well, these city officials were shocked and angry. And so it began.

They wanted us to gut the building completely, and put in every imaginable fire protection. The whole project would cost twice as much than what we had paid to purchase the building. At the time, this was an insurmountable amount. They advised me to take the church out of the city. They didn't realize was that we serve a big and rich God. The Lord financed the remodeling, and we did not get into debt. They had no choice but to give us the certificate of occupancy. In that year of persecution, the church experienced a mighty revival, and we increased with many new members.

When people see that you serve with excellence, they give freely and liberally out of gratitude!

In 1992, I was elected as the District Superintendent of the Southeastern, Spanish District of the Assembly of God, now called the Florida Multi-Cultural District. The offices, at the time, were in the previous Superintendent's garage. The Treasurer told me, there was no money. The District was broke. The night I was elected, my wife and I went to a place near the convention where there was a lot of street entertainment. We saw this clown doing some tricks and telling jokes. Every five minutes, he would pass the hat for people to tip him. Hardly anyone gave. Some people dropped some coins when he pleaded for tips. I told my wife that I hope he had a day job, because he was going to starve to death. We continued to walk, and there was a young man that looked like he was in his 20's playing piano. He had everyone dancing and enjoying his awesome talent. On his piano, he had an empty fish tank. The people would fill the tank with money. He never asked for a dime, but people would give with joy. He would have to stop playing the piano to empty the fish tank, and then continued. The Holy Spirit spoke with clarity in my heart. "Many churches are like that clown, but if my people are given excellence, they will give abundantly." I met with all the District leaders and instructed them to just call the pastors, and serve with excellence and joy. Within two years, we bought a piece of land and built the District offices. God supplied, and the people gave abundantly. When people feel that you serve with excellence, they give freely and liberally out of gratitude.

The ministry should not be burdened by lack of finances.

God will always supply for His kingdom, as long as we are doing His will. We must learn to hear His voice, and do His will. I have seen God's provision throughout my life. As an Evangelist and Pastor living without a steady income, millions of dollars have passed through my hands to be a blessing to others and His kingdom.

My wife had a vision when we were starting the church that I am presently pastoring. We were facing a challenging time. We were purchasing a $1.8 million building with zero money. We were a bit concerned, to say the least, and she said that she heard in this vision what Christ told Peter. "The money is in the mouth of the fish" (Matthew17: 27). In other words, don't worry about finances, just win souls, and then they will give. Don't put the cart before the horse; it's about souls not buildings. My building fund has been to increase our missions giving. The more we give to missions, the more He provides for the church.

As long as you are obedient to His direction, you will walk under His provision.

He is your source. He will supply according to his riches in glory. Always keep your motives pure. Do all for the glory of God. Never compete with other churches. Resist the urge to be the biggest church in the city or the best. Keep in mind, God wants to bless all those that call upon his name. You should always pray for all the churches and pastors in your area.

A Note of Warning: There needs to be transparency in the church finances.

You should never have a family member as the Treasurer. You should never handle the church's money. Have an open-book policy. Have an independent audit on a yearly basis. Let everyone in the church feel free to look into the financials. If there is a safe in the church where money is deposited, the Pastor should not know the combination. The safe should not be in the Pastor's office. This will protect you in case of fraud. Also please Pastor, do not live beyond your means. Learn to live accordingly (Hebrew 13:5).

> *"But they that are minded to be rich fall into a temptation and a snare and many foolish and hurtful lusts, such as drown men in destruction and perdition. For the love of money is a root of all kinds of evil: which some reaching after have been led astray from the faith, and have pierced themselves through with many sorrows. But thou, O man of God, flee these things; and follow after righteousness, godliness, faith, love, patience, meekness."*
> 1 Timothy 6:9-11 (ASV)

If you get into personal debt, you will cause pressure on your family and the church.

Have high-integrity in your finances. When people see this, they give without hesitation. Large donors are successful because they are wise with their finances. Before they give large donations they observe how the institutions are using their finances. If they see anything that is dubious they will withhold their donation.

Transparency in the finances of the church will protect you from any criticism and false accusations. It will also inspire people to give of their hard-earned money. They must have no doubt that their offering is being used wisely. You must be very cautious with the finances of the church.

Trust and Finances

What are your thoughts about this chapter? What stood out? What areas need to change?

Chapter 19
The Anointing

There is no other method of living piously and justly, then that of depending upon God.
JOHN CALVIN

The Anointing Breaks the Yoke

> "The Spirit of the Lord is upon me, because he anointed me to preach good tidings to the poor: He hath sent me to proclaim release to the captives, And recovering of sight to the blind, To set at liberty them that are bruised, To proclaim the acceptable year of the Lord."
> Luke 4:18-19 (ASV)

I've realized that anointed preaching gets to the point. It's clear and speaks to the heart of the listeners.

Anointed preaching brings spiritual awareness of the presence of Jesus in the midst. His Holy presence brings conviction of sin, hunger for God, and an overwhelming knowledge of His love. When the anointing is absent, you talk and talk, and can't quite say what you want to say. You take longer than necessary, and don't quite get to the point. It's not life-changing, and produces no permanent fruit. It might even entertain, but it's forgettable. Anointed preaching is edifying to the mind and spirit. It gives clarity to life's problems and brings conviction, and demands application in the hearts of those that hear. It produces thirst for more.

What is anointed preaching?

It's preaching with conviction and compassion. It's having a word birthed by the Holy Spirit in prayer. The scripture teaches us that Christ would spend many hours in prayer before the Father. He inspired his disciples to want to pray. He taught them that we should ask God to give us so that we can pass it on.

> *"And he said unto them, Which of you shall have a friend, and shall go unto him at midnight, and say to him, Friend, lend me three loaves; for a friend of mine is come to me from a journey, and I have nothing to set before him; and he from within shall answer and say, Trouble me not: the door is now shut, and my children are with me in bed; I cannot rise and give thee? I say unto you, Though he will not rise and give him because he is his friend, yet because of his importunity he will arise and give him as many as he needed."*
> Luke 11: 5-8 (ASV)

I will never forget my first pastorate. Here I was, a 19 year old who knew very little Spanish, was recently married, still in Bible School and pastoring a Spanish church. I had to speak in Spanish and give a decent message every Sunday. I was so nervous, and felt so inadequate. This made me spend hours, prostrate before the Lord. I would pray at least 5 hours a day. In-spite of my inexperience and lack of Spanish, we had many give their hearts to Christ. The atmosphere was inundated with the presence of God. The members noticed this, and got excited about what was happening. They started bringing visitors. The church exploded. It grew, and we moved to a bigger building. Jesus would heal and deliver many. The glory of God was present in all our gatherings. All of the sudden, pastors would call me so that I could give seminars on church growth. They would ask me, "What was the method I used for church growth?" I didn't have a clue. For the life of me, I was completely unaware as to "What was the method?"

I pastored that church for 10 years from 1971 to 1981. The Holy Spirit led my wife and me to full-time evangelism. In 1985, the Lord led me to West Palm Beach where I founded a church called Love Tabernacle, now known as "International Tabernacle." At first, it was a struggle. I felt like I knew how to "do this." I had a successful pastorate already, so I felt confident. It wasn't going too well. The Holy Spirit whispered in my heart, "If you approach this ministry as you did as a young, inexperienced-preacher, and spend time in prayer, you will see the same results."

Yes...that's it. There is no secret formula or method. It's being in His presence. It's to humbly walk before the Lord, and depend on Him at all times. It's giving Him all the glory and honor. This will keep your heart broken for the lost, and will keep you hungry for God.

One important item in your daily agenda is to get alone with God, to seek his heart, and to intercede for those that the Lord has put before you.

The church pays you to pray and spend time in the word. Truly you are blessed. All other things should wait. Give priority to your devotional time. Do not become a professional reverend. If you preach and pastor without a prayer life, you have become arrogant. My dependence on God draws me to prayer. Prayer and fasting places me in the blessings of God, and causes me to be a blessing.

The church must be called or known as a "House of Prayer" Matthew 21:13

The church in Yonkers was a praying church. They would have all-night prayer services almost every Friday, and fast on Sundays. Many try to imitate the programs of other growing churches, and sometimes after great excitement, came great disillusionment.

How many pastors leave the ministry feeling like failures, when some program that worked for others didn't work for them? It's like when David tried on Saul's armor. It just didn't fit. It's not the program that made it work. It was the anointing of the Holy Spirit. Many of us want to imitate

Pastor Choi in Korea's cell group ministry, but don't imitate them in their prayer discipline. They have over ten thousand members praying in church every morning, and every Saturday, they fast and pray for the Sunday message.

One day I decided to announce to the community, that we would have an open-door service, where everyone would be welcomed. We emphasized that, no matter what your religion or lifestyle was, we would pray for the sick and demon oppressed. We announced it in all the media. The church started fasting and praying for that service. Needless to say, when the day came, we never had so many visitors; mostly unchurched. You could imagine my elation. I preached a gospel message, and to my surprise, hardly anyone responded. Well I got upset, and thought of not praying for any sick and bound, but I swallowed my religious ways, and I invited all that wanted healing and deliverance to come forward. The whole crowd came forward.

We formed many prayer lines, and divided them among the Elders and Deacons of the church. There was an explosion of miracles. Many were miraculously healed and delivered. Afterwards, we would ask them if anyone wanted to give their hearts to Jesus, now that they saw His power, and they would.

Two miracles stand out. One of them was a young lady that despised me. She had an ardent, adherence to a certain religion that spoke against our church. She was very upset because many of her family members had gotten converted in our church. When she would see me walk by, she would cross the street to avoid me completely. But, she needed healing and therefore, she went that night. When I saw her, she looked very upset at having to be there before me. I remember telling her that if she wanted her healing, she had to lift both hands and praise the Lord in an audible voice. (I did this just to bother her because I knew how much she just wanted to get out of there...pronto.) As she lifted her hands rather hesitantly, I laid hands on her and asked God to give her a special blessing. As I was praying, she fell and hit the floor real hard. It was so hard that the whole congregation let out a gasp. I was scared too because I thought she got hurt, and that she would surely sue me. She was out for a while, and I proceeded to pray for the others on line. After about 15 minutes, she stood up and was crying. I approached her and knew that God had done something powerful in her life. She proceeded to tell the congregation that as she was prayed for, she floated to the floor like a feather. The whole congregation started laughing, because we all heard the thud when she hit the floor. Then she said, as she laid there, she opened her eyes and saw angels; and if angels were in our church, then she had to be there to. She gave her heart to Jesus right there.

Another miracle that stood out was a man that had come with only one kidney. The doctors had taken out the other kidney, and told him that the one he had left was malfunctioning. He would soon lose that one too, and would have to start doing dialysis. He testified two years later that when he left the healing service, he went back to the doctor. The doctor was shocked when he discovered two healthy kidneys.

Preaching is also prophetic utterances.

Be true to your outline, but be open to a sudden prompting by the Holy Spirit. One day, I was preaching in a very large church in Orlando, FL. They were broadcasting the service on a radio station. All of the sudden, I said something unplanned and out of context. I raised my voice and said, "You, who are thinking of suicide this moment, God loves you and has a purpose for your life. Stop and desist from taking your life." Then, I continued with the outline and totally ignored what I had said. Seven years later I was preaching in another church, and a Deaconess shared her testimony. She shared that seven years ago, she had found out that her husband had been having an affair. She ran into her car to commit suicide. When she turned on the car, she heard the radio transmission of the service. At that very second, she heard my voice and said, "You who are thinking of suicide, God loves you and has a purpose for your life. Stop and desist from taking your life." Praise God for His love, grace and mercy.

The anointing is a supernatural ability to do God's work. It enables you to do what otherwise would be impossible. It breaks demonic holds. When the anointing flows, your ministry becomes effective in transforming lives. It will deliver those that are captive and will share biblical revelations.

When you are ministering under the anointing, you are an efficient, well-oiled machine.

Eddie Rodriguez

What are your thoughts about this chapter? What stood out? What areas need to change?

Chapter 20
Healing Beliefs

*If it is the will of God for man to be sick,
no one in history violated
the will of God more than Jesus.
Just as God desires all men to be saved,
He also desires all men to be healed.*
JOHN GOODREADS

Does God want to heal all the sick?

The bible clearly teaches that every good gift, and perfect gift, comes from the Father of lights (James 1:17). It also shows a merciful God when Christ walked on the earth. Jesus came to manifest the true nature of the Father. He healed the sick and delivered the demon possessed. He forgave sins, and restored what Satan had stolen. The scriptures are very clear on this subject.

Some say that if He wants everyone healed, why doesn't He heal everybody? That same argument can be used against salvation, but that doesn't change God's will. Scripture says; *for God wills that none should perish, but that all should come to repentance (2 Peter 3:9).* Are all going to be saved? Not at all, nevertheless, this is God's perfect will. So it is, with

His will to heal and deliver all those that need a miracle.

As a preacher of the gospel, you must preach God's perfect will for all.

When I preach, I believe that everyone that hears this gospel will be saved. I believe God wants to save all of them. When I pray for the sick, I pray with that same conviction. I believe God wants to heal everyone.

This is very ironic, coming from me. In my family, we confronted death and disease in a very real way. I had the privilege of being raised in a Christian home. My dad was a minister of the Gospel, and a pastor of a beautiful church in Manhattan in a section called Harlem. It was a Spanish church where the people prayed and sang with all their passion. I had two wonderful brothers, Nelson and David. What great singers they were. They were blessed with powerful and anointed voices. Nelson Jr. was the oldest. David was the middle child, and I was the youngest.

One day, my parents decided to go Puerto Rico to visit our grandparents. We were four, five, and six years old. While in Puerto Rico, everyone noticed that we were falling constantly, and they urged my father to take us to the doctors. Well, the diagnosis was that we all had Muscular Dystrophy. What a shock to my parents. I can still hear my mother wailing and weeping on that fateful day. They were so proud of their three children.

When my mother would take us out for a walk at Riverside Park in Manhattan, people would ask if she was the nanny. You see, we did not look like the stereotypical, Puerto Ricans. We had platinum blond hair with very light skin and green eyes. Our childhood was filled with great New York City memories (like stick ball, roller skating, tops, hide-and-seek and home-made, race cars with milk cartons); and now, my dad and mom were faced with this prognosis.

My dad shared that he went to church and asked God to grant him the blessing of having at least one child without this dreaded disease. When they took us back to the hospital, the doctors said that I did not have Muscular Dystrophy. I was miraculously healed. I don't know why my father asked for just one. These mysteries are left to God.

The first one to go with the Lord was David. It was during a youth prayer meeting. That evening, the youth of the church had gone to the altar to pray. During this time, both my brothers, could not walk, and were confined to a wheelchair. David, the middle child, asked me to take him to the bathroom. As I waited for him I asked "David if you were to die right now, would you go to heaven?" He answered me, without hesitation that he would most assuredly go with God. I was taken aback by his conviction. I rolled him back towards the altar, and I went back to pray. As I was praying, I started to ask God to heal him, but I couldn't. What came out of my mouth was a prayer that I did not want to say. "Lord, take him in glory." I would then stop myself, and tried to ask the Lord to heal him, but what would come out of my mouth would be "Lord, take him in glory." At that moment, everyone in the church felt an overwhelming presence. We all started praying in the Spirit and crying before God. All of the sudden the glory left and we all got up from our knees and looked around. We knew something supernatural had taken place. When I looked toward my brothers, David had left to be with the Lord. I truly believe that God's angel came down, and took him when we felt that glorious presence.

My other brother Nelson was devastated. He could not understand why God would take him. He was told by well-meaning brothers that maybe God wanted him with that sickness. This caused my brother Nelson to rebel. He said that he wouldn't wish or want this sickness on anybody, and if God wanted him sick, he wanted nothing to do with Him. He became an atheist.

My brother and I would argue for hours. He denied the existence of a soul. He went on to study, and got his Masters and then his Doctorate. One day as I was visiting with my parents, my mother entered into the living room crying. She said that my brother, Nelson, was dead. I ran into his room and saw his lifeless body. I called the ambulance, and when I went back to his room, he was alive. He was crying and looked at me and said "Eddie, remember when I said that the soul does not exist? Well, I died and I left my body. I didn't know where I was going. God has given me a second chance."

From that day forward, my brother lived for God. He went on to live for another three years. He loved seeing God heal the sick. He told me never to say that God wants people sick. Even though he never received his healing, he died confessing it and seeing it from afar (Hebrew 11:13). He knew that God would heal him. If not now, He would in the resurrection. He also knew that the glory which awaited him was far greater than his present suffering. He told me many times, that he looked forward for the resurrection. He knew that he would be raised in the last days without Muscular Dystrophy and that he would have a new body likened unto Christ's.

Before he got saved, my brother wrote a poem that became well-known to express his grief. He was invited to the Muscular Dystrophy Association to take part in their yearly telethon, and was interviewed by the host of *Good Morning America*, Mr. David Hartman. He was asked to explain his poem.

An Existence Without Life
Nelson E. Rodriguez

I think therefore...I exist
With an Inquisitive, Intelligent mind...I exist
Incarcerated not behind bars of steel
But in a lifeless body...I exist

With a heart full of dreams;
Mirages in a desert
Messages written in the sand

Healing Beliefs

*Erased by the breezes and the tides of the ocean
Like the sand in my fist they vanish
My reasons for living*

*An existence without life?
A question whose answer I never find
Why do I just exist?
This secret so guarded as if it were behind
The sacred veil of sanctuary*

*Golden Carousel;
Among laughs
I seek my desire,
My wish...to find a reason to live*

*It's like a having a hope
Which will never be realized
It's like a burning coal
Its warmth and color attractive
To one in need of its comfort
But in its attraction one is betrayed
By the pain of its holding
and soon death...
So much like love*

*Cursed chess game
Full of uncertain moves
The reply, Check Mate!
The end of the game
In anxious moments
A cruel joke*

*A fountain of pain and pleasure
Like Don Quixote with the lance in hand
I go to conquer non-existent castles
It's my conflict in life the real vs. the ideal*

*Maybe my windows aren't covered
with trickling rain drops*

Eddie Rodriguez

But the windows of my soul
Are covered in Mist
Without life...I exist
Can someone please tell me why...I just exist?

In it, he wrote of his frustration of existing but not living. He explained to the host of Good Morning America that he lived across the street from a High School, and he would stare out the window and see the kids ride their cars, go out on dates, play sports and do all sorts of things that he couldn't. He felt that he did not have a life. He just existed. But, he went on to share that he had written that poem before he had a life-changing experience. You see, he said, "I thought that life was doing things and I was miserable and wanted to die. Then I met Jesus Christ, and I realized that now I have life. I am filled with joy and hope and now I know I have life."

He would go to my crusades, and if I didn't pray for the sick, he would ride his electric wheelchair to the stage and yell out "Eddie pray for the sick." He was adamant in his conviction that God was against sickness, and that God is a good God.

As a preacher of the gospel of Jesus Christ, just preach what is said in the scriptures.

Don't form a theology based on emotional or personal experiences. Whether your experiences contradicts the revealed truth or not, the truth is not what you feel or see. It is what is revealed in Christ Jesus.

Prayer for the sick and demon possessed is important for church growth. The gifts of the Spirit are powerful and loud bells that call sinners to repentance. You should experience the same results today that Christ had when He walked the earth with His physical body. The multitudes flocked to Him. They will flock to Him today, if we let him be who He is; a healer and deliverer.

Divine healing is a direct mandate from our Savior. It's a blatant disobedience to ignore it.

What are your thoughts about this chapter? What stood out? What areas need to change?

Chapter 21
God of New Things

*Man cannot discover new oceans,
unless he has the courage
to lose sight of the shore.*
ANDRE GIDE

> *"Thus saith Jehovah, Stand ye in the ways and see, and ask for the old paths, where is the good way; and walk therein, and ye shall find rest for your souls: but they said, we will not walk therein."*
> Jeremiah 6:16 (ASV)

This is one of the most misunderstood and misused verse in the Bible. This verse is referring to the principles of our theology. Not the methods or the workings of God. He says, "I will do new things, things that you will find it hard to believe."

> *"Remember ye not the former things, neither consider the things of old. Behold, I will do a new thing; now shall it spring forth; shall ye not know it? I will even make a way in the wilderness, and rivers in the desert."*
> Isaiah 43:18-19 (ASV)

> *"Behold ye among the nations, and look, and*

> *wonder marvelously; for I am working a work in your days, which ye will not believe though it be told you."*
> Habakkuk 1:5 (ASV)

The church needs to work, not out-of-the-box, but without a box. Think about how creative God is. Not one snowflake is the same. There is no limit to His creativity. He says that, ear has not heard, nor eyes seen the things God has for His people.

> *"But as it is written, Things which eye saw not, and ear heard not, and which entered not into the heart of man, whatsoever things God prepared for them that love him."*
> 1 Corinthians 2:9 (ASV)

Our imagination falls short before God's will for you.

> *"Now unto him that is able to do exceeding abundantly above all that we ask or think, according to the power that worketh in us,"*
> Ephesians 3:20 (ASV)

Albert Einstein is broadly credited with exclaiming, "The definition of insanity is **doing** the same thing over and over again, but **expecting different results.**" There are methods of ministry yet to be discovered. We must be open to these awesome possibilities. God has a different key for every city and generation.

Every member has a ministry.

You will be surprised at the ideas your members will come up with, if you teach them this principle. Let go of the old so that God can replace it with the new. He will pour new wine into new wineskins.

> *"Neither do men put new wine into old wineskins: else the skins burst, and the wine is spilled, and the skins perish: but they put new wine into fresh wine-skins, and both are preserved."*
> Matthew 9:17 (ASV)

The members of the church I pastor have come up with ministries, within the church, that have surprised even me, ministries that have produced many awesome results. God's will is that all be filled with his Holy Spirit, which will result in prophecies, visions and dreams.

> *"And it shall come to pass afterward, that I will pour out my Spirit upon all flesh; and your sons and your daughters shall prophesy, your old men shall dream dreams, your young men shall see visions:*
> Joel 2:28 (ASV)

My church team has developed ministries specific to their needs and past wounds.

Examples:
1. Ministry to parents with handicapped children
2. Ministry of Bereavement for those that have lost a loved one

As society experiences different things, God will raise up specific ministries.

As you journey in this calling, my prayer is that your heart will be open to God's purpose for you. It is also my prayer that you will not short-change yourself and live excited, expecting God to do new things through you.

Believe God so that you can be the happiest pastor on earth; and that the ministry that God has given you, can experience His all.

If you're one of those ministers that have left the ministry, God's calling and gifts are still upon you. That priestly robe is still on your life. It may be stained and shattered, but it's still there. He wants to lift up your head, place you on a higher plain, and put a new song in your heart. Forgive yourself, and continue your journey. It's never too late. So pick up your cross, deny yourself and go.

This whole book is summed up in these three words; in order to live and have a successful ministry, you need to have Love, Humility and Obedience.

Eddie Rodriguez

Bon Voyage!!!

*As I look back over fifty years of ministry, I recall innumerable test, trials and times of crushing pain.
But through it all, the Lord has proven faithful, loving, and totally true to all His promises.*
DAVID WILKERSON

What are your thoughts about this chapter? What stood out? What areas need to change?

About the Author

Pastor Eddie Rodriguez has served as evangelist since 1967. He was a street preacher in New York City and still enjoys preaching on a street corner besides holding mass evangelism crusades in all of Latin America, Asia and Europe. He has pastored and founded churches in New York, Florida and Paraguay. He started the pastorate at 19 yrs. old in 1971 and has enjoyed a fruitful ministry. Has served as District official of the Assembly of God since 1987 as General Presbyter, Assistant Superintendent and Superintendent. He has served in the board of administration at Southeastern University in Lakeland, FL, as well as many other national boards. He is presently the founding pastor of A Place Called Hope in West Palm Beach fl. He is married to Martha since 1970 and has 3 children and 7 grandkids.

You can contact Pastor Eddie at eddierodriguez212@yahoo.com

References

Barna.com; Barna: Pastors; Research Releases

www.ingramcontent.com/pod-product-compliance
Lightning Source LLC
LaVergne TN
LVHW051556070426
835507LV00021B/2602